Lost Dublin

Frederick O'Dwyer

Gill and Macmillan

First published 1981
Second impression 1982
Third impression 1985 by
Gill and Macmillan Ltd
Goldenbridge
Dublin 8
with associated companies in
Auckland, Dallas, Delhi, Hong Kong,
Johannesburg, Lagos, London, Manzini,
Melbourne, Nairobi, New York, Singapore,
Tokyo, Washington
© Frederick O'Dwyer, 1981
7171 1249 7
Design and Origination by Healyset, Dublin
Printed in Hong Kong

CONTENTS

To Daniel Gillman,
and in memory of Sylvester Gillman,
who documented the passing of Old Dublin

INTRODUCTION

Lost Dublin is intended primarily as a record of buildings, now gone, erected since 1700. Some have long since been demolished, others will be remembered as if they had disappeared only yesterday. Many of the photographs, including some copied from lantern slides, are reproduced for the first time. Some are the only known illustrations of the buildings concerned while others show rare street views and interior details.

The opening section is devoted to O'Connell Street — the heart of the city. Succeeding chapters are based around a journey starting in the south city centre and travelling outwards in an anti-clockwise direction taking in the area around College Green and Dame Street and going east to Nassau Street, to St Stephen's Green and then back across the river via Butt Bridge, the old Gardiner Estate and surrounding areas — to the east, north and west of O'Connell Street and spreading to take in Glasnevin and the Phoenix Park. We then recross the Liffey to St James's Gate and travel eastwards through the Liberties to the old city centre around Winetavern Street and the neighbourhood of St Patrick's Cathedral and Dublin Castle. The next three chapters deal with the south east city and selected buildings in Dun Laoghaire and the south suburbs, and a further selection from the north east suburbs including Clontarf and Santry. The final chapter is a collection of some remarkable designs that never made it past the drawing board.

I wish to express my thanks to the following people for their help: Maurice Craig, David Davison, Séamus de Burca, F. E. Dixon, Michael Duncan, Clifton Flewitt, William Garner, Daniel Gillman, David Griffin, Kieran Hickey, Edward McParland, Kevin Murray, John O'Connell and Peter Walsh. I would also like to thank Margaret McGahan of Bord Fáilte; Noelle Nathan of Hospitals Trust, Dublin; Patrick Johnston, curator of the Dublin Civic Museum; William O'Sullivan, keeper of manuscripts, Trinity College, Dublin; Nicholas Sheaff, archive director and the staff of the National Trust Archive; and the librarians and staff of the Royal Irish Academy, the National Library of Ireland and the College of Technology, Bolton Street. My special thanks to Bill Doyle who skilfully copied and enlarged details from old postcards, engravings and early photographs.

Author and publishers wish to thank all those who gave their help in providing illustrations; sources are acknowledged below, and after the relevant page number, one of these abbreviations, indicating the illustration's position on the page, may be found — t (top), c (centre), b (bottom):
Patrick Abercrombie with Sydney and Arthur Kelly, *Dublin of the Future, the New Town Plan,* vol. 1, Civics Institute of Ireland 1922: p. 144t and b; Allied Irish Banks: p. 24b; Bord Fáilte: pp. 22, 24t, 53, 54t, 60t, 65b, 66c and b, 75b, 83b, 90b, 95b, 104c and b, 105t, 122b right, 128; Trustees of the British Museum: p. 5b; S.F. and H. Brocas, from a print: p. 18t; W. Brocas, Junior, from a print; p. 97t; *The Builder:* p. 134b; Maurice Craig: pp. 57b, 65t, 72t, 73b, 75t, 78b, 88b, 89t, 99t, 114c, 118b; Séamus de Burca: pp. 61b, 69, 74t and b; Deegan-Photo Ltd, Dublin: pp. 41t and b, 46b; F. E. Dixon: pp. 25t, 127t; *Dublin Builder:* p. 64; Dublin Civic Museum: pp. 28b, 29b, 85b, 91b, 106t and

c, 108b, 124c; G. A. Duncan, Dublin: pp. 10, 15b, 17c, 23t, 25b, 30t and b, 52t, 60b right, 66t, 77, 80t, 99b, 119t, 121t and b left, 122t; Georgian Society Records: pp. 56b right, 78t—author's drawing from a plate, 109t; Gillman Collection: pp. 3 right, 9b, 14 right, 31b, 33t, 39b left, 43b from Brooking's Map (1728), 45, 47b, 48, 49t, 55b left, 56b left, 61t, 67t, 83t and 86—7t from Brooking's map, 88t, 93t, 94t and b, 96b, 98b, 117t and b, 118t, 123b, 128b, 129t, 131b, 133t, c left and right, 135, 136t, c and b, 137 from Brooking's map, 145; Green Studio Ltd, Dublin, courtesy of Trinity College, Dublin: 138t right; Guinness Museum, Dublin: 95t, 96t; National Trust Archive: pp. 4b, 6t, 7t and b, 12, 18t right and b, 20b, 28t, 38t, 39b right (Irish Georgian Society Collection), 40t, 62, 68c, 71 (Irish Georgian Society Collection), 84b left and right, 89b, 110c, 113t and c, 114t, 115, 124b, 132b, 139t, 140b, 141t and b, 143t, 145b, 146; Irish Architectural Records Association: p. 111t, b left and right; *Irish Builder:* pp. 6b left and right, 26b, 29t, 34, 35 left, 70, 112, 120, 126b, 140t; Hospitals Trust, Dublin: pp. 9t, 80b, *Irish Times:* pp. 3 left, 4t, 17t and b right, 19b, 20t, 31t, 42t left, c and b, 52b, 58, 59t, 60 left, 98t, 108t, 114b, 122b, 125, 126c, 134t, 143b; Patrick Jammet: pp. 33b, 36t left and right, b, 37t; Lensmen, Dublin: p. 1; Uinseann MacEoin: pp. 38b, 57t, 87b; Municipal Gallery of Modern Art, Dublin: p. 142; Kevin Murray: 139b; National Library of Ireland—Lawrence Collection: pp. 4c, 11t, 15t, 21, 23b, 26t, 35 right, 39t, 40b, 44t—detail enhanced by George Morrison, Dublin, 47t, 49b, 50, 63, 67b, 68t and b, 74c, 82t, 84t, 85t, 90t and c, 91t, 93b, 100b, 101t and b, 103b right, 105b, 110t and b, 116t and b, 121b right, 126t, 127b, 129b, 130t; Derry O'Connell, *The Antique Pavement,* Dublin 1975, courtesy of An Taisce: p. 82b; Tony O'Malley Pictures Ltd, Dublin: pp. 51t and b; Peter Pearson: p. 119b; Pieterse-Davison International Ltd, Dublin: p. 76t; Robert Pool and John Cash, *Views of the Most Remarkable Public Buildings, Monuments and other Edifices in the City of Dublin,* Dublin 1780, courtesy of the National Trust Archive: pp. 85c, 109b, 124t; Royal Society of Antiquaries of Ireland: pp. 5t, 8, 11b, 13t, 14 left, 27, 55t, and b right, 59b, 72b, 73t, 87c, 92t and b, 100t, 102t, c and b, 103b left, 104t, 106b, 107c and b, 118b, 130b, 132t; Sir John Soane's Museum, London: p. 138t left; John Topham Picture Library, Edenbridge, Kent: pp. 2, 16, 56t; Peter Walsh: pp. 54b, 97b, 103t, 107t.

I

O'CONNELL STREET

The foundation stone of NELSON PILLAR was laid by the Lord Lieutenant, the Duke of Richmond, on 15 February 1808, a little over two years after the admiral's death at Trafalgar. The design was furnished by William Wilkins (1778-1839), the London architect, but superintended in its erection by Francis Johnston (1760-1829). The 134 ft high doric column cost £6,857 to build, £3,000 of which had been raised by the merchants of Dublin by the end of 1807.

The Portland stone for the 13 ft high statue was supplied by the committee, and the Cork sculptor Thomas Kirk was paid £300 to carve it. Kirk (1781-1845) also carved the statues of Hibernia, Mercury and Fidelity over Johnston's General Post Office, a building which in the architectural sense complemented the Pillar.

By 1878 some public representatives were calling for its removal as a traffic hazard. Alderman Peter MacSweeney proposed that it be re-erected in a city square. In 1891 Thomas Sexton MP, later Lord Mayor, introduced a bill in the House of Commons proposing removal. He was supported by Tim Healy and T.D. Sullivan but strongly opposed by the Unionists who carried the day. Years later, W. B. Yeats described the Pillar in the Seanad as 'that monstrosity that destroys the view of the finest street in Europe'.

On the night of 7 March 1966 the upper half of the column was shattered by an explosion. The remainder was blown up by army engineers two days later.

These TWO TRAMS on O'Connell Bridge were photographed about 1944 — note the absence of other traffic on O'Connell Street. The first car No. 193, here on the 15 route to Terenure, was built at the Spa Road works and entered service in July 1925. No. 108, behind it, was of a later design and first left Spa Road in September 1934.

Both were repainted in the Dublin United Transport Company's new green and cream livery in 1942. The Terenure route closed in November 1948 and the tramway system in July of the following year.

THE CAPITOL CINEMA, Prince's Street, was originally opened in 1919 by Messrs F. W. Chambers and George P. Fleming as the La Scala Theatre and Opera House, the name being included in the terracotta decoration on the facade. T. F. McNamara (1867–1947) was the architect while L. G. Mouchel and Partners of London designed the reinforced concrete frame.

With three tiers of private boxes and two cantilevered galleries the theatre could seat fourteen hundred spectators. In addition there was a ballroom, cafes, lounges, meeting and social rooms and a garage. The premises extended to Middle Abbey Street where La Scala Buildings occupied Nos. 83–6. The Capitol closed its doors in March 1972.

The former Cinerama in Talbot Street became the New Capitol for a period until its demise in August 1974. The Prince's Bar which stood next door to the Capitol was built at about the same time for the Tierney family to the designs of John J. O'Hare. Like the Metropole and the Capitol it was demolished to make way for the new BHS department store. Portions of its pink Aberdeen marble counters were re-erected at the Sutton House Hotel and at a new pub, the Henry Grattan in Lower Baggot Street, where many of its fittings may also be seen.

3

THE METROPOLE Cinema, Ballroom and Restaurant opened in 1922 on the site of the old Metropole Hotel which had been destroyed in the Rising. It was designed by Aubrey V. O'Rourke (1885–1928), less well-known perhaps than his brother Horace (1880–1963) who, as city architect, was responsible for planning the new O'Connell Street, although in fact Aubrey was quite prolific in designing many city buildings including the Dolphin's Barn Synagogue and Moran's Hotel.

The old Metropole at No. 37 Lower Sackville Street was a hotel as early as 1834, when it was Spadaccini's. It was later the Prince of Wales Hotel under Mrs Elizabeth Smith, proprietress. It was subsequently sold to the Jury brothers who operated up to 1892 when it was purchased by the Mitchell family who employed their kinsman William Mansfield Mitchell (1842–1910) as architect on an elaborate reconstruction of the hotel which included the addition of much ornate ironwork, including a verandah serving the first, second and third floors and a canopy extending out over the pavement. It was the Mitchells who first adopted the name Metropole.

The new cinema and ballroom then had a lifespan of just fifty years. During that period it was one of the most fashionable places of entertainment in the city and the venue for several civic functions. It was demolished in 1973.

HOTEL METROPOLE, SACKVILLE ST. DUBLIN. 4818. W.L.

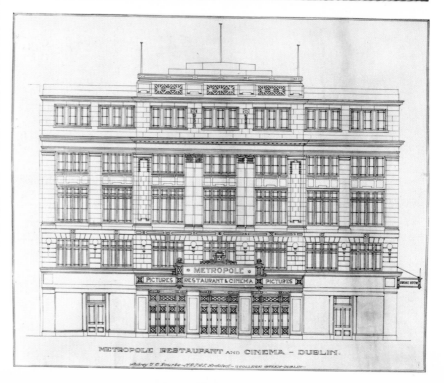

METROPOLE RESTAURANT AND CINEMA - DUBLIN.

4

Two views of UPPER SACKVILLE STREET (now UPPER O'CONNELL STREET): The photograph was taken in the 1890s from the top of Nelson Pillar. The etching, which was made in the early 1750s by Oliver Grace, artist and client of Richard Castle (c.1690–1751) who designed several houses in the street, reads: 'This street was begun by the Right Honble. Luke Gardiner Esq. in the year 1749, it's in Length 1050 feet, in Breadth 150, its Breadth is equally Divided into three parts, in the midst is the Mall in Length 800 feet in Breadth 50....'

Some of the houses may be conjectural, although a later (1756) version of the print, with corrected perspective, differs little architecturally. One readily identifiable building is Drogheda House, six bays wide, in the second block on the right-hand side, which is discussed below. Gardiner had acquired the former Moore estate from the trustees of the Earl of Drogheda in 1714. He demolished the houses on both sides of the upper part of Drogheda Street between Henry Street and Great Britain (now Parnell) Street, and widened it westward, to create the new Sackville Street, named after Lionel Cranfield Sackville, Lord Lieutenant from 1731–7 and 1751–5.

5

ENTRANCE TO MESSRS GILBEYS 87 SACKVILLE ST

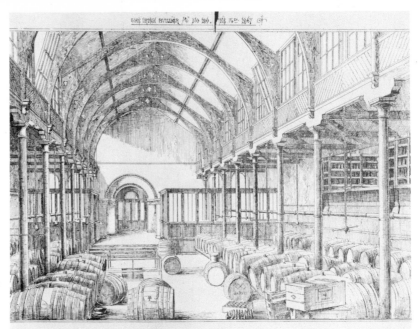

THE IRISH BUILDER Vol No 20. June 15th 1867

INTERIOR OF MESSRS W & A GILBEYS' STORES, SACKVILLE ST.

In 1865–7 the wine firm of W. & A. GILBEY tore down the fronts of Nos. 46 and 47 Upper Sackville Street, and erected a new Romanesque façade — Suffolk brick with Portland stone dressings and capped with a French chateau crested roof. The architect, William George Murray (1822/3–1871), also built extensive warehouses to the rear.

A feature of the façade was the elaborate porch, with Connemara marble shafts and inset busts of Palmerston and Gladstone who had reduced the tax on wine. Behind Murray's façade, the principal rooms of the 1750s houses were retained. They had been occupied from an early date by the wine merchants Sneyd French and Barton, and already boasted extensive cellars.

Gilbey's occupied the first and upper floors of the reconstructed buildings, renting out the ground floor to the newly established Etna Insurance Company. With the removal of Gilbey's to the suburbs in the early 1970s, the O'Connell Street premises was put on the market and was purchased for redevelopment.

The busts of the prime ministers were salvaged and given to the National Gallery. The adjoining houses Nos. 48 and 49 were also demolished. The fine eighteenth-century front drawingroom ceiling of No. 49 (part of which building was once used as a store by Messrs Gill, publishers) was taken down, and, following a chequered history, has now been re-erected in a house in Co. Wicklow, under the supervision of Mr Jeremy Williams. Some fragments, including the putti centrepiece, have alas been lost.

7

NO. 54 UPPER O'CONNELL STREET was built by Major Carleton Whitelock, an army agent, on a lease of 1752. For much of the nineteenth century it housed the Dorset Institution 'for the relief of industrious females'. In 1798 the Rev. James Whitelaw described it as a 'vacant barrack'. The Friendly Brothers of St Patrick had their clubhouse here for some years from 1820.

The principal feature was the back drawing-room which the Georgian Society Records surmise held the Van Dycks seen by Mrs Delany at Whitelock's former residence in Henry Street in February 1751. The bow window was flanked by richly carved wood pilasters with corinthian capitals. It was demolished when the Carlton Cinema expanded in the late 1920s.

This AIR RAID SHELTER at the top of O'Connell Street, photographed in 1940, was painted with advertisements for the wartime Red Cross sweepstakes organised by the Hospitals Trust. Note the gap to the left of Butler's Medical Hall, where the premises at the corner of Parnell Street had been taken down, pending rebuilding, in the previous year.

THE RICHMOND NATIONAL INSTITUTION FOR THE BLIND moved to No. 37 Upper Sackville Street (later No. 41 Upper O'Connell Street) in 1811, two years after their foundation in nearby Great Britain (Parnell) Street. According to the Georgian Society Records which illustrated two fine ceilings and a mantelpiece in the house, it was built by the Rt Hon. Benjamin Burton, MP for County Carlow. The arcaded ground floor was inserted in 1876 when the premises were remodelled by the architect J. Rawson Carroll (1830–1911). Both No. 41 and its neighbour No. 40, which served for some years as Aer Lingus offices, were pulled down in the late 1960s to make way for the Royal Dublin Hotel. No. 40 had been built about 1753 by the architect Nathaniel Clements (1705–77), Ranger of the Phoenix Park and Master of the Game, and remodelled in 1869 by Thomas Newenham Deane (1828–99) for a firm of bedstead manufacturers.

Messrs ALEX FINDLATER & CO. LTD, wine merchants and grocers, photographed here at the time of their closure in the late 1960s, were among the oldest businesses in O'Connell Street and had branches throughout the city and suburbs. Their first appearance in the directories was in 1828, when they were at 8 Burgh Quay.

By 1835 they were established in Upper Sackville Street, as it then was, at No. 27, later renumbered No. 30. By the 1870s they had expanded to take Nos. 29 and 31 and later took in No. 32 also.

The adjoining street, now Cathal Brugha Street, was named Findlater's Place in 1882. The Dublin Artisan's Dwelling Co., of which William Findlater was a director, built houses here and named one of their new streets Findlater Street (off Infirmary Road) after him. The corner building, No. 28 O'Connell Street, damaged in the Civil War, was rebuilt in the uniform style chosen for the street by the city architect, Horace O'Rourke. These buildings were replaced by a new office block in the 1970s.

Practically the entire east side of UPPER O'CONNELL STREET was destroyed during the first week of July 1922 when the buildings, occupied by the Irregulars, were bombarded by Government troops. These buildings included several hotels: the Gresham (Nos. 21 and 22), the Crown (No. 18A), the Granville (No. 17), and the Hamman Hotel and Turkish Baths (Nos. 11—13).

Other premises destroyed were Mackey's Seeds (No. 23), the temporary GPO (Nos. 14—16) that was opened after the Rising, the Hibernian Bible Society (No. 10), formerly Drogheda House, and the Tramways Office (No. 9) (qq.v.).

The Gresham Hotel was opened in 1817 by Thomas Gresham, in what had been three houses dating from the early 1750s. Nos. 15 and 16 were said to have been built from the designs of Richard Castle for Robert Handcock MP, of Waterstown, Co. Westmeath, but had been greatly altered in the nineteenth century. The staircase of No. 15 is illustrated here. No. 18, described by the Georgian Society Records as the only remaining authenticated example of Castle's work on the street, was built in 1750 for Henry Bellingham of Castlebellingham, Co. Louth.

Some of the houses on the opposite side of the street, occupied by Government troops, were also destroyed in the battle, as was St Thomas's Church (q.v.) in Marlborough Street.

THE SAVOY CINEMA was, at the time of its completion in 1930, the largest in
Ireland with seating for three thousand, having been redesigned during the planning stage to suit 'talkies'. It was designed by London architects, Messrs Mitchell,
and built by Messrs Meagher and Hayes of Cork and Dublin who also developed
several of the adjoining sites.

This section of Upper O'Connell Street had been destroyed in the Civil War.
Nos. 16 to 18, the last section of the Savoy complex to be built, were not
completed until 1936.

The auditorium was an escapist tour-de-force in the best traditions of Hollywood, with rich fibrous plaster decoration by the Dublin firm of Alex Malcolm
and Co. The Moorish baroque streetscape on the walls framed a Venetian pro-
scenium arch based on the Ponte di Rialto, beneath which the Doge's Palace
and Canale di San Marco shimmered on the backdrop.

Alas, the auditorium was drastically remodelled in the 1960s and subsequently
subdivided to create three cinemas.

12

The finest house on Sackville Street (now O'Connell Street) was DROGHEDA HOUSE, which had a frontage of 66 feet and extended back 180 feet. Its name dated back to 1771 when it was purchased by Charles, 6th Earl of Drogheda, for £5,000.

It had been built, however, by Alderman Richard Dawson, a wealthy banker, on a lease from Luke Gardiner dated 30 May 1751. Originally six bays wide, it appears to have served also as Dawson's counting-house, probably with a business entrance at the side on Stable Lane, as only one door is visible in Oliver Grace's view (see page 5). This view shows interesting finials on the parapet. The counting-house theory comes from the fact that it was subsequently divided as Nos. 9 and 10, and although the latter was demolished in 1866 for T. N. Deane's Scottish Provincial Assurance office, the surviving portion appeared, when examined by the Georgian Society, to be a 'complete dwelling-house'.

Although the architect of Drogheda House is unknown, the Knight of Glin has suggested that it may have been built by John Ensor from designs made by Richard Castle who died in February 1751. The rather exuberant plasterwork, however, does not suggest Castle's work.

In 1824 No. 9 passed into the hands of William Curry, the music publisher, who sold it to the Scottish Provincial. The new building, described as 'sixteenth century Scottish and based on the French baronial of that period', may have been designed by J. J. O'Callaghan (d.1905) who worked in Deane's office up until 1871. It was later sold to the Dublin United Tramways Company.

During Easter Week 1916 all the buildings from O'Connell Bridge up to Earl Street were razed. No. 10 somehow survived, its corner turret marking the limit of the destruction. It survived only a further six years. In July 1922 both it and Drogheda House proper were among the many houses in the street badly damaged in the action between the Free State Army and the Irregulars. Bibles stored in Drogheda House (the offices of the Hibernian Bible Society) are said to have been the first items ignited in a blaze that swept along the street through holes knocked (for communication) in the party-walls by the rebels. The remains of Nos. 9 and 10 were pulled down with hawsers.

13

Among the landmarks destroyed in the Rebellion was the IMPERIAL HOTEL, on the right in the photograph, which occupied the upper floors of Nos. 21–7 Lower Sackville Street. The hotel was started in 1837 by one Richard Moore Esq. and regularly changed hands. It was acquired from the Lawler family by Clery & Co. in 1902.

One of the new directors was William Martin Murphy, proprietor of the *Irish Independent* and director of the Dublin United Tramways Co. It was from one of its balconies that Jim Larkin made his celebrated address, during the 1913 'lock-out', at a meeting that ended with his arrest and with the crowd being baton-charged.

The ground floor of the hotel was occupied by Messrs Clery & Co.'s department store. This business began in 1853 as McSwiney & Delany's and was acquired by Clery's in 1884. The present store was built on the site in 1919–22, Clery's having been housed in the interim in the Metropolitan Buildings, Lower Abbey Street.

Between 1850 and 1853 RICHARD ALLEN, woollen importer and clothier, replaced his conventional premises at No. 28 Lower Sackville Street with a long galleried shop based no doubt on London examples. The façade was, in the Dublin context, highly unusual and reminiscent of a triumphal arch with corinthian columns and caryatids framing a three-storey high window. It was destroyed in Easter Week 1916.

14

DUBLIN BREAD COMPANY, Lower O'Connell Street, was built in 1901 by James Beckett, contractor, to the designs of the youthful George F. Beckett (1877–1961). The building was constructed on a steel frame and clad in brick with Portland stone dressings. The first floor was occupied by the luncheon room. The tops of the bay windows served as balconies for the smoking-room on the floor above.

Although the façade was erected with a central subdivision — supposedly to harmonise with the other frontages — the building totally dominated the street. The huge tower gave commanding views over the city, rivalled only by those obtained from its near neighbour, the Pillar. The feature was not universally popular; the Company had to raise the chimney flues of the adjoining buildings to overcome draught problems. It was gutted during Easter Week and subsequently torn down.

THE GRAND CENTRAL CINEMA, 6–7 Lower O'Connell Street, was opened in 1920 as the D.B.C. Picture House, on the site of the former D.B.C. restaurant (q.v.), and had a relatively short lifetime, being sold to the Hibernian Bank in 1949.

As with many other cinemas of the day, the premises also housed a restaurant. The glass canopy was removed when the building was remodelled by the Bank. Note the helmeted policeman on traffic duty.

15

The view from Nelson Pillar looking south over LOWER O'CONNELL STREET shows the extent of rebuilding following the Rising. The entire east side from North Earl Street to Eden Quay was destroyed. On the west side practically all the buildings between Bachelor's Walk and Middle Abbey Street survived, the destruction being largely confined to the block between Abbey Street and the GPO.

II

SOUTH CITY CENTRE

THE BOWL OF LIGHT: As part of a campaign to attract exiles back for a vacation, a series of events including religious ceremonies, processions, pageants and parades were planned to take place throughout Ireland in April 1953 under the title of An Tostal – Ireland at Home.

Dublin's contribution included the erection of a structure on O'Connell Bridge, unveiled on 5 April to reveal a rectangular fountain with concrete walls and urns and, as a centrepiece, a plastic flame – 'The Bowl of Light' – raised on tubular steel arches. This was soon dubbed 'The Tomb of the Unknown Gurrier' by Jimmy O'Dea. The flame, which appears to have operated on the same principle as a coal-effect fire, was hurled into the Liffey by a group of undergraduates a fortnight after its erection. The fountain was subsequently drained and turned into a flower-bed, known as 'The Thing'; it survived well into the 1960s when the Corporation were persuaded to reinstate the lantern sets that had first graced the bridge in 1881.

The façade of the old Corinthian Cinema, remodelled in the 1960s, can also be seen in the photograph.

THE CARLISLE BUILDING AND THE BALLAST OFFICE: The Brocas engraving 'View from Carlisle Bridge', published in 1820, shows the vistas down Westmoreland and D'Olier Streets, begun in 1800 by the Wide Street Commissioners and culminating in the quays in a formal composition. The Carlisle Building stood on the left, the Ballast Office on the right, and a smaller though matching building stood in the angle.

Bush, writing in 1769, noted that the first Luke Gardiner had intended to have a grand public building on this site to terminate the vista across the river from an extended Sackville Street. However, nothing happened until 1782 when the Commissioners sought a grant for a new river crossing, made possible by the commencement of the new Custom House downstream of the projected line from Sackville Street to the Parliament House.

A map was published about this time, presumably by the Commissioners, showing 'the Improvement of the Eastern End of the Town by opening the streets and building a New Bridge over the River'. It shows a crescent-shaped piazza on the southern bank with a central statue and three radiating streets.

'A New Plan of Dublin' published by the City Surveyor, Samuel Byron, seven years later, shows a similar proposal but with only two radiating streets. The more westerly was on the line of Fleet Alley, a narrow laneway.

While work on North Frederick Street and the south end of Cavendish Row got under way in the 1780s, it was not until 1790 that funds were set aside for Sackville Street, and it was 1792 when plans for Westmoreland Street were sought.

Only with the diversion of a clubhouse tax in 1799 did funds reach the Commissioners to proceed with the latter. Three schemes were produced by the architect Henry Aaron Baker (1753—1836) for the Commissioners' surveyor Thomas Sherrard. The first proposal had a colonnaded ground floor enclosing the pavement with shops behind. The second was a formal palatial composition without the colonnades, and the third very much as executed — four storeys above ground-floor shops. It was among the earliest purpose-designed shopping streets in these islands.

Of the three buildings at the apex, Carlisle Building, No. 28 D'Olier Street was the grandest. It had three upper floors to its neighbours' four, five bays to Burgh Quay and six to D'Olier Street. The name plaques, one with the owner's name — Kinahan Son and Smyth — were in place as early as 1820. Messrs Kinahan & Sons, wine and spirit merchants, continued in occupation into this century with the Commissioners of Irish Lights as tenants of the upper floors. Until the mid-1920s it was the head office of Independent Newspapers and after the completion of their Middle Abbey Street premises it served as the advertising office. It was demolished in the early 1960s to make way for O'Connell Bridge House.

The building in the angle of D'Olier and Westmoreland Streets was greatly embellished by the London and Lancashire Insurance Company in the 1870s and was demolished in 1894 when they erected a new baronial gothic pile by J. J. O'Callaghan. Because of its prominent position it was nicknamed 'O'Callaghan's Chance'. To later generations it was known as 'Purcell's Corner' after the ground-floor shop.

The third building, the Ballast Office, No. 21 Westmoreland Street, was erected by the Corporation 'for Preserving and Improving the Port of Dublin' in 1802. The Aston's Quay elevation was five bays wide, and that of the Westmoreland Street façade three. In 1864—5 the building was remodelled both internally and externally under the superintendence of the architect Charles Geoghegan (1820—1908): a balustrade, quoins and window architraves were added. In 1866 the adjoining three-bay premises Nos. 19—20 (there were two shops at ground level) was destroyed by fire. The shell was taken down and the Ballast Office extended, Geoghegan's treatment being continued although he had been replaced by John McCurdy (1823—85). The work which was completed in 1868 included a new entrance and boardroom. The marrying of new and old was not entirely successful, the presence of a substantial party wall between the buildings making for a tortuous plan.

In 1870 the clock was installed, connected to a time signal for mariners on the parapet. The chief component of this was a copper sphere which dropped down a wooden shaft each day at 10 a.m. For some years the clock was regulated via cable by a master clock at Dunsink Observatory.

The building was sold when the Port and Docks Board moved to new premises in 1974. It was demolished in 1979 to make way for a modern office block, with replica façades above ground-floor level. The clock was salvaged for re-erection on the Aston's Quay front.

D'OLIER STREET was laid out after 1800 by the Wide Street Commissioners with five-storey over-basement houses of generally uniform width and design. No. 24 was designed in 1820 as the Dublin Library, by George Papworth (1781—1855). It was erected at a cost of £5,594. It was reconstructed in the 1930s in the art deco style for the Gas Company, by the architect J. J. Robinson (1887—1965), who rebuilt the adjoining Leinster Market.

In 1883 T. N. Deane and Son remodelled Nos. 21—24 for the Junior Army and Navy stores, uniting the buildings with a reconstructed ground floor with large plate-glass windows set between rusticated piers capped with a modillion cornice. The establishment did not long survive Independence and was vacant for some years before being bought in 1926 by Messrs T. & C. Martin, who employed William H. Byrne and Son as architects for further alterations. D'Olier House, as it had become known, was sold in 1968 and was subsequently demolished and replaced by an office block of the same name.

While much of WESTMORELAND STREET remains essentially as it was when laid out in the early 1800s by the Wide Street Commissioners, some infill took place in Victorian times and some since. The corner buildings on the east side, to the south of Fleet Street, Nos. 35 and 36, were replaced in 1936 by the neo-classical Pearl Insurance Company building (now a bank), designed by A. F. Hendy (1894–1958).

On the opposite corner the 1920s terracotta-faced, steel-framed EBS building, Nos. 33 and 34, was replaced in the 1970s, although the old frame remains, encased in concrete, behind the new mirror glass façades. The rich terracotta façade of the Paradiso which was built about 1912 for the photographers Lafayette, to the designs of Fuller and Jermyn, has been kept in a scheme completed in 1981 which involved the demolition of the Irish Times and Graham's (q.v.), Nos. 31 and 30. The Irish Times clock has been preserved and awaits re-erection in D'Olier Street.

GRAHAM'S PHARMACY, No. 30 Westmoreland Street, which closed in June 1975 had a fine Greek revival double-storey interior decorated with anthemions, corinthian pilasters and classical statues. The shop front on the other hand was art nouveau dating from 1912.

The premises were in continuous use as a pharmacy from 1821, being owned for many years by John James Graham and latterly by three generations of the Walsh family. The building, together with Nos. 29 and 31 (the Irish Times), was demolished in 1978.

20

THE TIVOLI THEATRE, Burgh Quay, had its origins in Daniel O'Connell's Conciliation Hall, built in 1843 as a meeting place for the Repeal Association. An English visitor in 1846 described it as a 'large, new building, very plain, but quietly elegant and commodious, and extremely like a very large chapel of the wealthiest class of our Dissenters in England'.

It was lit by lunette windows, set high in the otherwise blank walls. On the ceiling were 'three very large and beautiful rosettes of pale green and gold containing the shamrock in low relief, with a harp in the one in the centre'.

By the 1870s the Hall had become the corn and flour store of Messrs Macmullen Shaw & Co. The Dublin Corn Exchange, probably built after a design by Robert Smirke (1780–1867) was next door. In 1896 the architect William Henry Byrne (1843/4–1917) was commissioned to convert the premises into a music hall. The rere and side walls were retained and an elaborate new front topped by a statue of the Goddess of Music added. Into the interior, he inserted a horseshoe shaped auditorium with gilded baroque plasterwork and surmounted by a dome. The contract was awarded to Michael Meade. Work was completed by the following year at a cost of £20,000. At first called the Grand Lyric Hall, the name was later changed to the Tivoli Theatre of Varieties.

In 1930 the building was acquired by the directors of the newly founded Irish Press who commissioned T. J. Cullen (1880–1947) to draw up plans for its conversion to offices and printing works. Much modified in recent years, of the original fabric only the rusticated ground floor is now visible.

The first THEATRE ROYAL on the Hawkins Street site was opened on 18 January 1821 by Harris, patentee of the London Theatre Royal. The premises, which had been lately occupied by the Royal Dublin Society, was extensively remodelled by the leading English theatre architect Samuel Beazley (1786–1851). A proposed elaborate façade with an ionic loggia illustrated by Petrie in a contemporary print, was never executed. The auditorium, horse-shoe shaped, reputedly seated in excess of two thousand.

In 1880 the building was destroyed by fire, the conflagration starting when a faulty gas jet in the viceregal box was being lit prior to a performance. The proprietor, Michael Gunn, who had built the Gaiety Theatre nine years earlier, employed the London architect C. J. Phipps (1835–97) to design a new music-hall for the site. The Leinster Hall opened on 2 November 1886 and closed finally in 1897 when it was sold to a syndicate.

The building was remodelled to the designs of Frank Matcham (1854–1920) as the new Theatre Royal. Among the artists to appear there in this century were McCormack, Paderewski and Kreisler.

It was torn down less than forty years later when yet another theatre was built. The architect was Leslie C. Norton of London while the executant architects were Messrs Scott and Good of Dublin. The third Theatre Royal and adjoining Regal Rooms (the latter on the site of the former Winter Gardens) were opened on 23 September 1935 by the late Sean Lemass, just sixteen months after the closure of the old Royal.

The exterior was in what we now know as the art deco style while, according to the souvenir programme, 'A richly lavish Moorish architectural scheme has been adopted for the decoration of the auditorium which is based on authentic details from the Alhambra at Granada in Spain'. While the *Irish Builder* regarded the practice of spending money on such ostentation as 'rather dubious', their criticism, based on a supposed audience lack of interest in 'a sketchy and perhaps over busy reproduction of Arabian ornament . . . while yielding to the products of Hollywood or Elstree', was perhaps itself rather pompous.

The marble balustrading from the old Theatre Royal was incorporated in the new balcony, while other sections of the old staircase were relaid in the Regal Rooms. The Compton organ, installed in the auditorium and reputedly 'the largest and most modern theatre organ yet built', soon became synonymous with the name Tommy Dando.

The Royal featured 'cine-variety' with music, comedy, 'potted Shakespeare' from the Gate Company and Eddie Byrne's 'Double your Money' stage show. It had an even shorter life than its predecessors. The finale was held on 30 June 1962. The artistes on stage on the last night included Jimmy Campbell who had conducted the Royal Orchestra since the opening night twenty-seven years earlier; the Royalettes, choreographed by Babs da Monte and Alice Dalgarno; crooner Frankie Blowers; pianist Peggy Dell; and comedians Cecil Sheridan, Mickser Reid, and John Molloy. Some Royal personalities moved to the Gaiety, among them Jimmy O'Dea and Maureen Potter, while Jack Cruise moved to the Olympia. Within months of its closure the 'last' Theatre Royal was demolished to make way for an office block.

23

THE CRAMPTON MEMORIAL, better known to Dubliners as the 'Cauliflower', was unveiled at the corner of College Street and Hawkins Street in August 1862 in memory of Sir Philip Crampton M.D. (1777–1858) who served for many years as Surgeon General. Crampton was a keen naturalist, hence the botanical nature of the monument and its attendant swans; his bust nestled at the base.

A contemporary account of its erection stated that the sculptor, Joseph Kirk R.H.A. (1821–1894), hoped it would be a monument to himself as well as to Sir P. Crampton'. Removed by the Corporation in 1959, its departure was precipitated not by traffic plans as is often stated, but by the collapse of the upper two segments of the plant into the street.

THE ROYAL IRISH INSTITUTION, College Street, was erected in 1827–9 on part of the site reserved for the proposed Bank of Ireland (q.v.) some thirty years earlier. The architect was Frederick Darley, best known for the Magnetic Observatory in TCD (now removed to Belfield), the Merchants' Hall and the Library of the King's Inns.

The Royal Irish Institution 'for the encouragement and promotion of the Fine Arts in Ireland' was founded in 1813. Their first exhibition of Old Masters in the College Street premises was held in 1829. The site was awkwardly shaped, leaving many of the rooms with 'lozenge' plans. The main gallery on the first floor was in the shape of an octagon 40 ft long by 30 ft wide with a height of 19 feet to the cove, and was surmounted by a lantern light. The building was demolished in 1866 to make way for William George Murray's Provincial Bank.

JURY'S HOTEL: Among the projects instigated by the Wide Street Commissioners was the rebuilding of the north side of College Green and Dame Street. An elevational drawing dated 1791 and signed by Thomas Sherrard shows a terrace of thirteen houses — four storeys over ground-floor shops. A formal element was introduced with the treatment of the end houses with first and second-floor windows in a recessed panel of brickwork under a relieving arch.

While the project was never completed, a start was certainly made from the east end at Anglesea Street. The erection of Commercial Buildings stopped the westward progress of the terrace, only six houses being built. Jury's Hotel opened as Commercial Lodgings at No. 7 College Green in 1839. By 1849 'The Commercial and Family Hotel' occupied Nos. 6, 7 and 8, built on a Commissioners' lease of 1795, and Nos. 1 and 2 Anglesea Street. The founder, William Jury, was indeed himself a former commercial traveller. In 1866 he sold his interest to a cousin, Henry James Jury, who acquired further houses in Anglesea Street in 1874 and 1881.

While the premises were remodelled in 1859 (from the designs of E. H. Carson, 1822—81) and again in the 1880s, the main walls of the original houses survived. The formal façade of the corner house, No. 6, was altered to match the others, although the mark of the relieving arch and the panel beneath it was never successfully concealed in the new brickwork. The Jury family operated the hotel up until 1918 when it was taken over by the British authorities for office accommodation.

It was then empty for some years before being purchased by a group of Dublin businessmen in 1924. It then had seventy-seven bedrooms. Further additions (now Bloom's Hotel) were made in 1962. However, in 1973, following the acquisition of the former Intercontinental Hotel in Ballsbridge, the owners placed the building on the market and auctioned off the contents. The late Victorian Long Bar, latterly known as the Antique Bar, was sold as one lot to the General Bank of Switzerland and was re-erected at their premises in Pelikan Strasse, Zurich. It has been renamed the James Joyce Pub. Joyce had no known association with the hotel, although it is mentioned in *Ulysses*. Jury's was taken down in 1980.

COLLEGE GREEN. DUBLIN. 306. W.L.

Of Richard Johnston's grand ensemble of buildings, NOS. 1–5 COLLEGE GREEN, extending from Anglesea Street to Foster Place, only the lower three floors of the pillastered centrepiece of No. 2 survive. Part of the Foster Place elevation may be traced in the façade of the Allied Irish Bank.

The College Green centrepiece was designed in 1788–9 for Daly's Club, with a façade 63 ft in width. Johnston (1754–1806) was asked by the Wide Street Commissioners to extend the frontage to 138 ft with flanking houses designed to simulate wings to the Club, although these were intended for letting.

In 1791 the Club moved from 2–3 Dame Street into the new premises described as 'the grandest edifice of the kind in Europe'. In 1867 the right flank – Nos. 1 and 2 – were demolished by the Liverpool London and Globe Insurance Company, and were replaced by a new building designed by T. N. Deane as a neutral backdrop to the Bank of Ireland. Shortly afterwards the top floor of the former Club (which had closed some forty years earlier) was rebuilt and raised, and a balcony was added at first floor level although this has since been removed.

In 1880 Deane was called upon by the Royal Exchange Assurance Company to demolish No. 5, the surviving flank, which they had occupied for seventy-five years and to replace it with a dramatic gabled and turreted building in the Elizabethan style. Both Deane's buildings were demolished in turn in the early 1960s for modern office blocks. The centrepiece was again reroofed, and this time raised a further storey.

26

The oldest and long the only equestrian statue in Dublin was WILLIAM III, by Grinling Gibbons (1648–1721), in College Green, unveiled on 1 July 1701, the anniversary of the Battle of the Boyne. It was frequently mutilated. In 1836 the monarch was unseated by a bomb. Among the first on the scene was the Surgeon General, Sir Philip Crampton summoned by a message that an important personage had fallen from his horse in front of the Bank of Ireland.

The sculptor, John Smyth had to replace the head, a leg and the left arm — the new head being based on a bust by Van Nost. Chart observed in 1907 that 'The horse seemed quite unlike other animals of his race, and the rider despite his serenity of countenance did not look altogether at home in the saddle'. It was removed following an explosion in 1929.

COMMERCIAL BUILDINGS, DAME STREET: In 1794 a committee of Dublin merchants, opposed to the monopoly of the Royal Exchange, took a site on the north side of the street, ear-marked for redevelopment by the Wide Street Commissioners, where the General Post Office (which had moved to College Green in 1783) had stood. Two years later the foundation stone of the building 'for the general resort, and necessary accommodation of the Merchants and Traders of the said city' was laid.

The architect was Edward Parke, a protégé of John Foster, the speaker of the House of Commons and a Wide Street Commissioner. Dr McParland has noted that Parke's elevation derived from Chambers' Charlemont House. Commercial Buildings, which were opened in January 1798, were ranged around a courtyard backing onto Cope Street.

The court, which served as a short cut for generations of Dubliners walking from Dame Street to Merchants' Arch and the Metal Bridge, was up until 1888 also the venue of the annual November gathering of the Ouzel Gallery Society whose plaque, carved in Portland stone, stood over the south door. The Society, founded in 1705 to arbitrate in commercial disputes, was named for a ship thought lost to pirates in the Mediterranean but recaptured by its crew and returned to Dublin port in 1700 laden with booty.

Commercial Buildings were demolished in October 1970 to make way for the Central Bank Headquarters. The cut stone of the Dame Street frontage was numbered for re-erection but proved unusable. The elevation of a new building constructed on the east side of the plaza formed in front of the Bank is based on the original façade. The Ouzel Gallery plaque has been re-erected on the Dame Street front.

28

Another building that formerly stood on the Central Bank site was W. G. Murray's ROYAL INSURANCE OFFICE at the corner of Dame Street and Fownes Street, erected by Messrs Nolan of Meredyth Place in 1869. A typically sumptuous Italianate commercial palazzo, the Royal was faced with richly carved Portland stone relieved about the entrance by red, green and black Irish marbles.

At the time of the building's construction the *Irish Builder* reported: 'We understand that the "Royal" has made more progress in life and fire than any company yet established.' The interiors were elaborately detailed with 'masterly plaster-work' on the ceilings of the public office and first floor board room. The top storey was let out as offices, entered from a separate doorway in Fownes Street.

ROYAL INSURANCE BUILDINGS, DAME ST., DUBLIN.

CRAMPTON COURT off Dame Street was built about 1740 by Philip Crampton (1696–1792) a wealthy bookseller and sometime Lord Mayor of Dublin. Crampton acquired property in the area and lived in the Court himself. Nos. 17 and 18 had fine carved doors, one of which survived as late as 1965, by which time the houses had been reduced to one storey. All of the houses in the Court proper have now been demolished.

THE DOLPHIN HOTEL, Essex Street East, was built by the Nugent family in 1896—98 to the designs of J. J. O'Callaghan who was also responsible for Mooney's of Harry Street and pubs in Baggot Street, Manor Street and South Richmond Street. O'Callaghan, who had worked with Deane and Woodward in his youth, was a diehard Gothicist; the Dolphin was probably the last important secular building to be built in this style in Dublin.

During its heyday its restaurants and bars were much frequented by the legal and racing fraternities. In latter years this trade declined. The Nugents finally closed it down in 1966. Subsequent attempts at running the Dolphin as a public house were unsuccessful. Finally in 1979 after it had lain empty for many years work was begun on gutting the interior for conversion to offices.

PALACE STREET, off Dame Street, survived intact up until the late 1960s when the corner premises, Messrs Masons, was destroyed by fire. The adjoining properties and those on the Dame Street side of the block were compulsorily acquired by the Corporation and demolished in the late 1970s for road widening, leaving just one building, No. 2, standing on the west side.

This is the Sick and Indigent Roomkeepers' Society, founded in 1790 for the relief of the poor of all religious denominations and claimed to be Dublin's oldest charity. It too is scheduled for demolition.

NO. 34 DAME STREET was occupied by the Swift Cycle Company in Edwardian times. In the 1870s James Delany, merchant tailor, traded there. The façade is typical of the many Wide Street Commissioners' brick-faced houses which were remodelled in stucco in the early Victorian era. Shaw's Directory of 1850 illustrates how widespread this practice had become.

However, by the 1860s complete rebuilding, often in stone, became the vogue, particularly where insurance companies and banks were concerned. The history of No. 34 goes back to 1782 when designs by Samuel Sproule for this, the south side of Dame Street, were approved by the Commissioners.

In the 1960s No. 34 and some of its neighbours were refaced with a modern polished granite and glass façade by an insurance company which has since moved. The roofs and stacks of the old houses may be seen above what at first sight might appear to be a concrete-framed office block.

The NORTH BRITISH AND MER-
CANTILE INSURANCE CO. was
one of three Scottish firms to em-
ploy the Edinburgh architect David
Bryce to design their Dublin offices.
The North British was erected at
the corner of College Green and
Church Lane in 1855—66. According to the *Irish Builder* the façades
were based on Longleat House in
Wiltshire while Fiddes and Rowan,
in their catalogue note that Bryce
(1803—76) was influenced by the
staircase at Blois in the corner tower
and the François Ier style of the
overall design. The Dublin atmos-
phere did not prove sympathetic
to the Glasgow freestone with which
the building was faced. The company erected a substantial block at
the corner of Nassau Street and
Dawson Street about 1909 and
sold the College Green premises
to the post office. The building
was vacated on completion of
Andrew Street Post Office in the
1950s and demolished in 1975 to
make way for the Ulster Bank's
new headquarters.

Bryce's other Dublin buildings
— the Standard Life Office in
Upper O'Connell Street and Life
Association of Scotland Chambers
in Dame Street (later Craig Gardners)
— survive as the Northern Bank and
Trinity Bank respectively.

Among the longest established firms in College Green were MESSRS RICHARD ATKINSON & CO. who occupied No. 31 from 1835 (when they were described as 'Gold and silver tissue and tabinet manufacturers') up until 1958 when they were listed as 'Wholesale poplin manufacturers'. The firm was founded in 1820 and moved to College Green from No. 4 Cutpurse Row in the Liberties.

Richard Atkinson was Lord Mayor in 1857 and again in 1861. By that time Irish poplin had largely ceased to be used for dresses (Queen Victoria was a customer) and was being promoted for neck-ties. No. 21 was rebuilt in 1888–90 to the designs of Sir Thomas Drew (1838–1910). Atkinson's also occupied No. 2 Church Lane and had a weaving factory in the Merchant's Hall. In 1925 the firm opened the first of several factories in Belfast where production continues today.

No. 31 College Green was demolished in 1962 for an extension (by Beckett and Harrington) to the Ulster Bank which was in turn taken down in 1975 for their new headquarters. No. 30, seen to the right in the photograph, was stripped of its Victorian embellishments in the 1960s and was also demolished in 1975.

THE BURLINGTON DINING ROOMS AND RESTAURANT, 27 St Andrew's Street, achieved fame under the proprietorship of Joseph Corless whose speciality was oysters supplied from his 'Red Bank Oyster Beds, Burrin'. This is not to be confused with the rival establishment at 19 and 20 D'Olier Street, the Red Bank Oyster Hotel, run by Luke Waddock. The Burlington, or Gridiron, was established at 6 Church Lane by Henry Kinsley in 1829 in what had been a public house. Kinsley sold out to Corless in the late 1850s.

In 1876 the Andrew Street portion of the premises was rebuilt. In 1900 the restaurant was sold to two Frenchmen, Michel and Francois Jammet, who traded at 26—27 Andrew Street and 6 Church Lane until the late 1920s, when the lease reverted to their neighbours, the Hibernian Bank, who built a large extension to their head office on the site to the designs of Ralph Byrne (1877–1946). His work was much altered in the reconstruction of 1980—81 when the premises were remodelled for the Northern Bank.

THE SUN ALLIANCE FIRE AND LIFE offices at the corner of Andrew Street and Trinity Street were built in 1886 to the competition-winning design of George C. Ashlin (1837–1921) – a robust gothic edifice with crow-stepped gables and a conical tower at the angle – a favourite Victorian device for turning corners. Ashlin, who studied under Pugin and married his daughter, had the largest church practice in the country and did little commercial work. His only other insurance office – at the corner of Westmoreland Street and Fleet Street, also a competition winner – is perhaps judiciously Italianate rather than gothic, echoing the façade of Trinity College.

The Sun Life building later became the head office of the Phoenix Assurance Company and was subsequently acquired by the Northern Assurance Company. It was demolished in 1958.

34

III

NASSAU STREET TO ST STEPHEN'S GREEN

THE LAW CLUB, Nassau Street, was completed in 1870 to the designs of John McCurdy, the work being superintended on the Club's behalf by William Mansfield Mitchell. It was probably their first professional association — they later became partners.

The client was one of the oldest clubs in the city and the only one to commission a new premises in the gothic style. The Kildare Street Club (q.v.) had rejected Deane and Woodward's initial proposal for a gothic building twelve years earlier. It is interesting to note that the adjoining building, No. 26 (later No. 43) Nassau Street, had been designed by McCurdy in the Italianate style for Messrs J. S. Wilson in 1867.

One of the features of the Club façade (which indeed recalled much of Deane and Woodward's oeuvre) were the oriel windows of the first floor coffee-room and reading-room.

The premises were sold by the Club in 1884 to a razor manufacturer and were later acquired by Messrs Browne and Nolan who had previously occupied No. 46 Nassau Street, purchased in 1855. No. 46, later Jammet's (q.v.), is the only survivor of the three. In the mid 1960s the former Club and the Wilson shop were demolished (along with the Alliance Assurance Office (1904), No. 40 to the left of the Club, by Sir Thomas Drew, to make way for an office and shop development.

THE NEW LAW CLUB - NASSAU STREET

JAMMET'S RESTAURANT: When the lease expired on their premises at the corner of Andrew's Street and Church Lane in 1926, the Jammet Brothers acquired Kidd's Restaurant, 45—6 Nassau Street, and brought many of the old fittings with them. Michel Jammet, a native of Quillan in the Pyrenees, first came to Dublin as chef to Henry Roe, the distiller, but returned to Paris after several years. He was enticed back in 1895 by his appointment as chef to His Excellency Earl Cadogan, the Lord Lieutenant. In 1900 M. Jammet, in partnership with his brother François, purchased Corless's Burlington Restaurant (q.v.) in Andrew's Street.

François retired to Paris in 1908. Michel Jammet carried on until 1927 when he handed over control to his son Louis, who ran 'Dublin's only French restaurant' for almost forty years. Louis' wife Yvonne was an accomplished artist and sculptor, and a member of the White Stag group. Jammet's, however, was a meeting place not only for artists but also for literary and theatrical figures and Dublin business people.

Allegorical paintings of the Four Seasons, painted by an artist named Bossini allegedly to repay a debt, and originally hung in the Burlington, were ranged along the dining-room wall. At the rear, with an entrance to Adam Court, were the Oyster Bar and smoking-room. Upstairs were the Grill and Private Dining-room.

In 1946 a rather radical remodelling of the latter rooms was carried out under the superintendence of the architect Noel Moffet. The stained glass, plasterwork and panelling of the Grill were removed and replaced with a rather stark decor featuring exposed steelwork, plywood panels and curved glass block screens.

In 1967 Jammet's closed, marking perhaps the end of an era. While a restaurant continues to occupy the premises, unfortunately none of the interiors have survived.

The premises of MAGUIRE AND GATCHELL, sanitary engineers, in Dawson Street, demolished in 1978 after a decade of office use, encompassed a unique collection of architectural styles ranging from mid-eighteenth century to 1930s neo-Georgian. The latter, the block (Nos. 13–14) at the corner of Dawson Lane, was built from the designs of Harry Allberry (1872–1952). Next to it the nineteenth-century façade of No. 15 masked the town house of the Earls of Mayo built before 1761 by the first holder of the title, John Bourke, MP for Naas. It was sold in the 1790s to Richard Waller, solicitor. Three fine ceilings survived the various changes of use and were described in the Georgian Society Records.

Maguire and Gatchells began in 1837 as Maguire and Son, further down the street at No. 10, and later acquired No. 7 also. Two of the ceilings of No. 15 — those on the first floor — were saved by the developer and presented to An Taisce in 1978. The third, that of the ground-floor back room was salvaged by Mr Jeremy Williams and re-erected in another eighteenth-century house in the area.

One of the causes celèbres of Dublin architecture during the 1970s was the destruction of ST ANN'S SCHOOLS AND HALL. The schools were built in 1857—8 by Messrs Cockburn and Sons to the designs of Sir Thomas Deane Son and Woodward, and were described at the time as 'the first adaptation of the Early English style to street architecture' in the city.

The façade was polychromatic with alternate bands of calp and granite interspersed with red brick and Portland stone. The doorway and window heads were of creamy Caen stone. The internal arrangements consisted of 'schoolrooms for boys, girls and infants, 35 ft by 25 ft each, committee and classrooms as also apartments to accommodate eighteen boarders'.

In 1867, after the death of Benjamin Woodward (1816—61), T. N. Deane added the Molesworth Hall to the east, again polychromatic but in brick instead of stone. It was here that generations of Dublin girls attended dancing classes recalled by Elizabeth Bowen in 'Seven Winters'.

In 1974 the Minister for Local Government granted planning permission for the demolition of the schools and hall together with No. 45, a classical building in the style of Frederick Darley.

It was not until Easter 1978 that demolition work began. Following the destruction of the Hall and partial dismantling of the Schools, the site was occupied by architectural students for some days. The buildings were, however, repossessed by the contractors and torn down.

-HOUSE OF THE SPEAKER OF THE IRISH
HOUSE OF COMMONS, MOLESWORTH-ST.

MOLESWORTH STREET was laid out in 1727 by Richard, 3rd Viscount Molesworth and ran from Dawson Street where four houses were pulled down to make the connection to Coote Street, now Kildare Street. It was on the eastern side of Coote Street, in Molesworth Fields, that Lord Kildare, afterwards the Duke of Leinster, began his great mansion in 1745 with Richard Castle as his architect. Up to the 1880s when the present railings were erected by the Deanes, the view up Molesworth Street terminated in the rusticated gatehouse set between high walls which enclosed the courtyard of Leinster House. This feature was somewhat reminiscent of the arrangement at Burlington House in London, built in 1718–19.

In the photograph may be seen the arms of the Royal Dublin Society who moved here in 1815. The posters are for the Horse Show.

Of the twenty-three Georgian houses on the north side, only four survive, two on each side of Edward Holmes' (1832–1909) Masonic Hall of 1868. The pair to the west, Nos. 15 and 16, built by Benjamin Rudd, carpenter, have identical plans and were originally brick-fronted and gabled. The gable of No. 15 which was added in late Victorian times and was dated 1755 belies the origins of the house which Rudd sold to one Edward Deane of Terenure in 1740. No. 10, a public house, 'The Harp and Crown', in Georgian times, was occupied by John Bagwell M.P. in 1795 but had reverted to its former use by the mid nineteenth century. Rebuilt about the 1870s, it ended its days as Brian's Bar in 1972 when,

39

with Nos. 11 to 14 and Nos. 21, 22 and the corner house, it was demolished. The façades of these last three, built by George or Ralph Spring, were rebuilt in facsimile. No. 13, latterly the offices of Montgomery and Chaytor, had a fine doorway in a much mutilated façade. This house, the residence in the eighteenth century of the Rt Hon. James FitzGerald, Prime Serjeant in Ireland, is fully described in the Georgian Society Records. The ground floor windows were remodelled in the nineteenth century and the upper part of the façade rebuilt in the twentieth century. No. 14, which in 1744 was the residence of the Dowager Lady Masserene, appears to have been entirely refaced in the 1930s, with the top storey completely blanked off.

The two houses to the west of the South Frederick Street corner were replaced in the 1930s. The remainder on this side, including some with the gables masked, were demolished in 1978. The panelling of No. 3, built about 1727 by William Wilde, was particularly fine (see picture).

Of the twenty-four houses on the south side, those to the west of Molesworth Place were small houses built on the gardens of Dawson Street and taken down in the first half of the nineteenth century. The Molesworth Hall and other buildings built on their site are discussed above. Several of the remainder were rebuilt in the late Georgian style one hundred years or so after they first went up. Among these was the mansion occupied by Speaker Foster (originally No. 27), built pre-1740 and replaced before 1821 by the present Nos. 29, 30 and 31, of which an engraving survives. It was something of a hybrid, with gables on top of the parapet. The doorway was remarkably similar to that at Turvey, Donabate (q.v.). Only two gabled houses survive on this side, albeit with their gables rebuilt. Traces of early windows in a formerly gabled attic may be seen at No. 34 while No. 24, formerly Messrs Trueman's, retained its panelled interiors up to 1980. Lisle House, No. 33, described in the Georgian Society Records as the best preserved on this side, alas had its interiors removed in 1974. The fine carved staircase which they described as 'on the Jacobean plan' has been saved and awaits re-erection in another house in the city.

QUEEN VICTORIA MEMORIAL DUBLIN. 9646. W.L.

Perhaps the ugliest of the Dublin statues was that of QUEEN VICTORIA, which was executed in Paris by the Irish sculptor John Hughes (1865–1941) and erected in front of Leinster House in 1908 at a total cost of £7,320. The ensemble was designed by Sir Thomas Manly Deane (1851–1933). Flanked by statues of Erin, Peace, Fame and two wounded soldiers, the monument weighed a total of 168 tons. It survived until 1948 when it was removed at a cost of £6,500 to provide sixty-four parking spaces for members of the Oireachtas. It joined the remains of several other Dublin statues in store at the Royal Hospital, Kilmainham.

40

Perhaps the greatest loss to Dublin's Victorian heritage has been the destruction of the principal interiors of the KILDARE STREET CLUB in 1971. Following the sale of the northern half of the building by the Club in 1954, it was occupied for a number of years by an insurance company. While a 1967 application to demolish was refused, the absence of statutory control over interiors permitted the development company who eventually acquired the premises to remove the stair hall and erect mezzanines across the former morning-room and the drawing-room above it.

The Kildare Street Club was the last major building designed by Benjamin Woodward, who died in May 1861 some months before its completion. It was finished by his partner Thomas Newenham Deane. The grand staircase, with its elaborate pierced stone balustrades and dramatic spatial effects, probably derived from a design which Woodward had entered for the Whitehall Government Offices competition in 1857. Much of the beauty of the Club building lies in its carvings, the work of C. W. Harrison and others probably including the O'Shea brothers. While those on the exterior have survived, much perished with the destruction of the hall.

41

In August 1957 the last two houses in KILDARE PLACE, Nos. 2 and 3, were taken down. Controversy over their demolition led to the formation of the Irish Georgian Society. In 1884 there were four houses there: three on the east side and one, No. 4, on the south. This was the Model Schools of the Kildare Place Society which was erected in 1811. It was replaced by T. N. Deane's Church of Ireland Training College (q.v.), built in the 1880s. No. 1 was demolished at about the same time for the same architect's National Museum.

According to the Georgian Society Records, two large houses that had stood on the Museum site facing south, in the 1750s, (and leased by Lord Kildare), were pulled down prior to 1798. However, Roque's maps of 1756 and 1773 show only stables on this site. Nos. 1 and 2 were designed by Richard Castle for Lord Masserene and Sir Edward Skeffington Smyth Bart, respectively, and were executed after his death in 1751 by John Ensor.

Although visually linked by a common central stack and uniform window and parapet heights, Castle's treatment of each façade was quite different. No. 1 was relatively conventional – four bays wide with a pedimented door case in the third bay. In No. 2, however, in place of the outer two bays was a Venetian staircase window over the doorway, with symmetrical features on the two upper floors. No. 20 Kildare Street, which the Georgian Society Records attribute to Castle, has a similar façade. Although the Georgian Society records state that No. 3, which had a full height main stairs lit from both the roof and a Venetian window at the side, is later than Nos. 1 and 2, Roque shows three houses on the east side in 1756. A fine carved wooden mantle was salvaged from No. 1 by the Museum. A marble fireplace in the Adam style, formerly in No. 3, has been re-erected at Dublin Castle.

THE CAMPANILE, Kildare Place, served as the smoke stack for Government Buildings from 1915 until about 1972 when it was taken down. It was originally erected as the clock tower of the Royal University in Earlsfort Terrace in the 1880s (see photograph of Alexandra College q.v.) from the designs of Edward Kavanagh, Chief Draftsman of the Office of Public Works, under the supervision of J. H. Owen (1822–91). The clock dial and bell, originally at the GPO, were fitted in March 1887 by Messrs Frengley Bros. A second brass dial was added.

The Campanile was dismantled and re-erected at Kildare Place when the College was refronted by Professor R. M. Butler in 1915. The bell and dials remained propped against a wall in the College grounds up to the 1930s.

CHURCH OF IRELAND BUILDINGS, KILDARE STREET: In the autumn of 1811 the Society for the Education of the Poor of Ireland, soon to be known generally as the Kildare Place Society, was founded by a number of 'private gentlemen'. Between 1816 and 1825 college buildings were erected fronting onto Kildare Place and in the gardens behind. During the next fifty years the Society had a chequered career, Catholic Emancipation and the establishment of the National Board of Education having a pronounced effect on its fortunes.

Between 1854 and 1884 the Institution was run by the Church Education Society. In 1886 a new hall, the first of a series of buildings by T. N. Deane and Son, was completed. It was followed by a library and model classroom wing (on the site of the old pedimented schoolroom block). These were opened in February 1890 by the Lord Lieutenant, the Marquis of Zetland, who knighted Deane some months later on the completion of the nearby National Library and Museum.

The final phase, the recasing and reroofing, of the long block at the corner of Kildare Street was completed in 1907 by his son Sir Thomas Manly Deane. For over sixty years the Deanes' red-brick Tudor college stood opposite their stone-faced classical museum across Kildare Place. Later converted to office accommodation, the Church of Ireland Buildings were vacated in May 1968 and demolished two years later.

ST STEPHEN'S GREEN: This engraving, entitled *A Prospect of St Stephen's Green*, is taken from Charles Brooking's map of Dublin, published in 1728. The Green was not developed until after 1664 when the Corporation sold off 60 ft wide lots for building as a means of generating revenue. Some 27 acres at the centre of the Green were preserved as open space.

While the Georgian Society Records noted 'unfortunately there is nothing to indicate from which side the view is taken', comparison with Brooking's accompanying map and Roque's Map, published in 1756, would suggest that this is not the case. The position of the lodge in the bottom right-hand corner, in particular, would indicate that the view looks north.

While there was no doubt a certain amount of artistic licence in drawing the houses, those on the north side would appear to tally with the known positions of several important mansions. That on the top left corner, with the pyramid roof, was probably the residence of the Earls of Meath which can be traced back to 1702. It was demolished by Robert Smyth, the wine merchant, in 1830.

The large gabled house, with what appears to be a tower, coincides with the residence of Thomas Wyndham, Lord Chancellor from 1726 to 1739, marked on Roque's Map. Nos. 16 and 17 (the present Kildare Street and University Club) were built on the site about 1776. To its right is another gabled house, possibly that occupied before 1712 by Henry Petty, son of the cartographer Sir William Petty.

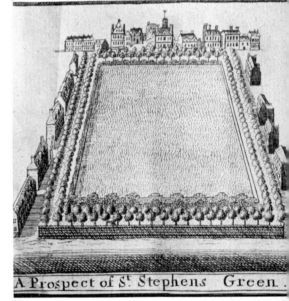

A Prospect of St. Stephens Green.

The next house shown coincides with the location of Kerry House on Roque's Map. It was occupied by Thomas Fitzmaurice, first Earl of Kerry, as early as 1722. He left it to his son Lord Shelburne. In 1793 the property was put on the market. It was acquired by Luke White in 1795, for £6,000, and let to the Government who used it as a military barracks.

Austin Cooper, the antiquary, went to the auction of the contents to see the 'State Bed so much talked of', an enormous affair with velvet curtains and head board embroidered with the Kerry arms. It brought £28. The house was accidentally burned some years later and Cooper recorded its demolition in March 1815.

Three houses built on the site were acquired, after 1820, by Martin Burke and converted into a hotel – the Shelbourne. The present hotel was built on the site in the 1860s from the designs of John McCurdy.

TRACTON HOUSE, No. 40 St Stephen's Green, was built by Arthur Jones Nevill, MP, Surveyor and Director-General of Fortifications, on ground taken from James Wilkinson of Corballis, Co. Dublin in 1744. Nevill was subsequently reprimanded for 'deficiencies in the barracks built under his directions' and expelled from the House of Commons. In 1752 he let the house to Richard Robinson, Bishop of Killala.

In 1765 the freehold was acquired by James Dennis, Serjeant-at-Law, made Chief Baron of the Exchequer in 1777 and created Baron Tracton in 1781. Tracton House remained in the hands of the Dennis family into the nineteenth century, but by 1831 had become a boarding house.

Within a few years it was divided into two as Nos. 39 and 40. In 1908 the northern portion, at the corner of Merrion Row, was greatly altered, the ground floor being converted into shops. Little original work had survived in the southern portion, apart from the back drawing-room. This was a panelled room with an elaborate rococo ceiling in one corner of which was scratched the date 1746. The centre-piece of the ceiling was a large figure of Apollo.

In 1912 the houses were acquired by the Bank of Ireland and demolished. The drawing-room, complete with ceiling, was taken down and presented to the National Museum where it was re-erected. It was later dismantled and put into store before being moved to Dublin Castle (q.v.) in the 1960s where it may now be seen among the State Apartments.

HUME STREET: The photograph of No. 45 St Stephen's Green was taken in the early years of the century when it was occupied by Nolan and Sons, antique art collectors and interior decorators, who traded under the name 'The Georgian House'. The name was something of a misnomer, for the house had been completely wrecked in the great storm of 6 January 1839 when it was the residence of Surgeon Thomas Rumley. According to the Georgian Society Records the damage was so severe as to necessitate its entire rebuilding. It would seem that the opportunity was taken at this time to build a house in the garden, No. 19 Hume Street, the gable of which can be seen in the photograph. In fact Nos. 17 and 18 Hume Street had been built in the same garden late in the eighteenth century. The laneway from Merrion Row behind the St Stephen's Green houses originally ran through to Hume Street.

No. 45, said to have been freestanding initially, had been built in its original form some time before 1741 when Sir Edward Bayly Bart of Plas Newydd, Anglesey, MP for Newry, was recorded as having been the occupant. The stuccoed house to the left, No. 44, was built by James Wilkinson, occupied as early as 1749 when Rev. John Echlin was the resident. The later history of Nos. 44 and 45 St Stephen's Green and Nos. 18 and 19 Hume Street is linked with that on the south side, Nos. 1 and 2 Hume Street and Nos. 46, 47 and 48 St Stephen's Green, in one of Dublin's most controversial planning issues. The last named were certainly more important as individual houses.

The corner house, No. 1 Hume Street, and the adjoining No. 46 St Stephen's Green were undoubtedly built simultaneously by the one developer, Gustavus

Hume. Hume (1732—1812), a surgeon who speculated in building lots, is known to have built the former, dated 1768 on a wall plaque, which he let in the following year to Richard Cox of Castletown, Co. Kilkenny, son of the Archbishop of Cashel. About 1900 the long flanking wall behind No. 1 Hume Street, long since the site of the last sedan chair 'rank' in the city, was removed and a three-storey eight-bay extension built in the garden to house the offices of the Commissioners of Intermediate Education. No. 46 St Stephen's Green was occupied in 1769 by one Dorothea Davis, widow.

No. 47 was built in the same year on ground taken from Hume by the architect John Ensor who let it to Redmond Morres, barrister, later MP for Dublin, while the contemporary No. 48 was built by another widow, Mary Thomas. No. 49 was built by Hume about 1771 and let in the following year to one William Dunn. In October 1966 the Green Property Company, incorporated the previous year, began demolishing Nos. 48 and 49, formerly the Dominican Hall, and its neighbour No. 47. At about the same time the lease of No. 46, held from the Green Property Company, and No. 1 Hume Street were offered for sale by the state. No. 2 Hume Street, formerly occupied by the Divine Word Missionaries, was acquired by the company towards the end of 1966, and Nos. 18 and 19 Hume Street and Nos. 44 and 45 St Stephen's Green in April 1967. Concern was expressed by conservationists that the entrance to Hume Street from the Green would be framed by modern buildings.

On 15 December 1969 workmen employed by the company began erecting scaffolding around No. 45, lately the offices of the Adoption Board, and commenced stripping the roof. Demolition was halted when the house was occupied by students of architecture from U.C.D., later joined by their fellow students from Bolton Street. Their action was supported by, amongst other backers, the Royal Institute of Architects of Ireland, An Taisce, the Dublin Civic Group and the Irish Georgian Society. While the students were evicted after several months' occupation, the company revised its proposals and over the period 1972—5 erected buildings with neo-Georgian façades.

This typical mid-nineteenth century Gothic revival church interior was that of the chapel of ST VINCENT'S HOSPITAL, St Stephen's Green, added in the 1860s and demolished just over a century later when the former hospital buildings, including the one-time residence of the Earls of Meath, were reconstructed and renovated for office use.

ST STEPHEN'S GREEN — SOUTH EAST CORNER: Between 1964 and 1971, the row of houses Nos. 65—76 St Stephen's Green were demolished for three separate office developments. One of the last to go, the corner house No. 65 occupied by Rosse College, was previously No. 66. The original No. 65 which adjoined it and three small shops Nos. 62—4 were demolished in 1839 when Earlsfort Terrace was driven through. The edge of the rebuilt gable wall of Rosse College can be seen clearly on the left in the photograph.

The most important house of the group was No. 76, built about 1750 and in this century occupied by Skerry's College. It was the residence from before 1752 of Thomas Le Hunte, barrister and MP for Wexford. Between 1784 and 1810 the owner was John Law, successively Bishop of Clonfert, Killala and Elphin, who moved here from York Street. The main feature of the house was the front drawing-room ceiling which has been salvaged by the Office of Public Works. The Georgian Society Records were critical of it, describing the plasterwork as 'a confused jumble of figures and ornament, an instance of the technical excellence and artistic defects of the rococo style in its decadence'. The principal subject of the ceiling was the four seasons but there were four subsidiary groups of figures as well as war and music trophy medallions. Curran thought the Georgian Society Records' judgment too severe and claimed to detect later insertions, as well as the work of two hands in the original.

WESLEY.COLLLEGE.DUBLIN.1638.W.L.

WESLEY COLLEGE, St Stephen's Green, was founded in 1845 as the Wesleyan Connexional School at No. 79 (now part of Iveagh House). George Bernard Shaw was a pupil in the 1860s. In 1877 Alfred Gresham Jones (1822–1915) who had been runner-up in the competition for the Belfast Wesleyan College, was asked to design a new college on the site of a livery stables behind the Methodist Centenary Church further along the Green. In the eighteenth century this site was occupied by Leeson's Brewery, leased after 1740 to the Sweetman family. Jones's spikey Victorian Gothic brick buildings were completed in 1879 at a cost of £20,000. Later additions included the stone-faced War Memorial Chapel by Beckett and Harrington. The College moved to Ludford, Ballinteer in 1972 and sold the St Stephen's Green buildings for development.

47

The RUSSELL HOTEL was first established at No. 102 St Stephen's Green as a 'temperance hotel'. Mr Thomas W. Russell had served as secretary to the Irish Association for the Prevention of Intemperance, and was later to become MP for North Tyrone. According to the Georgian Society Records the house was built about 1739 by Samuel Fairbrother, a stationer. Other sources suggest that No. 102, like its neighbours Nos. 103 and 104, was rebuilt in 1784 when Harcourt Street was opened.

By 1910 all three houses were occupied by 'Russell's Hotel'. The establishment was run for many years by Lady Martha Russell before passing into the hands of the Sedgewick family. In 1947 it was purchased by Mr Ken Besson of the Royal Hibernian Hotel, who took in a further house, No. 101. This house had been built in 1760 and sold in 1762 by William Fairbrother of Foxhall, Co. Wicklow to Dr Henry Quin, King's Professor of the Practice of Physic at Trinity College Dublin. The Quin family occupied it up to 1861. The brickwork was plastered and pediments added over the first-floor windows to relate it to the existing premises. The Robert Emmet Grill was located on the ground floor. The Russell closed in 1975 and was subsequently demolished.

THE WINTER GARDEN PALACE at the corner of St Stephen's Green and Cuffe Street was one of Dublin's more curiously named pubs. The original winter garden was a large glass and iron conservatory at the back of Alfred Gresham Jones' Exhibition Building, erected on Earlsfort Terrace in 1865 and removed in the late 1870s.

The house, No. 106 St Stephen's Green, or its predecessor, was the residence in 1778 of Godfrey James, attorney, seneschal of Kilmainham. During the nineteenth century it was occupied successively by an apothecary and two firms of chandlers before being opened as a public house by Philip Little who reconstructed the ground floor façade in terracotta and remodelled the interior with gilded ornament. It was occupied by the Volunteers during Easter Week but emerged from the fighting relatively unscathed. It was compulsorily acquired for road widening in the 1960s but was not demolished until the spring of 1975, having been boarded up in the intervening period.

STEPHENS' GREEN WEST. DUBLIN. 2235. W.L.

ST STEPHEN'S GREEN – SOUTH WEST CORNER: There were relatively few changes to the south-west corner of St Stephen's Green, from Cuffe Street to York Street, from the Lawrence era until the early 1970s. Today only W. H. Lynn's Unitarian Church, built in 1862 on the site of an early eighteenth-century mansion, and the pair of houses Nos. 119 and 120, attributed to Richard Castle, still stand.

Castle lived behind this block in Proud's Lane and apparently began building the new houses before his death in 1751. They were completed by Richard Thwaites who bought the site and materials on it in 1761.

Beyond them on the northern side of Proud's Lane stood the seven-bay breakfronted mansion of the Earls of Abercorn, the most important house on the west side, though in fact entered from York Street. This was subdivided into three in the early nineteenth century and further mutilated by the conversion of the ground floor into shops (Nos. 121, 122 and 122A) in Victorian times. It was the residence of the Abercorns as early as 1730 but at the end of the decade was rented to Robert Jocelyn, Lord Chancellor, who bought it outright in 1755. He was succeeded by his son who was created Earl of Roden in 1771 and who died in the house in 1797. The second Earl sold it five years later.

49

The bronze equestrian statue of GEORGE II was erected in St Stephen's Green in 1758. The sculptor John Van Nost the Younger (d.1787) settled in Dublin in about 1749 and received the commission in 1753. The monarch was depicted in Roman habit. In the 1930s the Royal Dublin Society, which had received its charter from George II, made two requests for the then unwanted statue. They were refused. It was blasted from its base one night in May 1937. A flower-bed now marks the spot where it stood.

The second monument in St Stephen's Green to be destroyed was a bronze statue of Archibald William Montgomerie, 13th Earl of Eglinton and Winton, Lord Lieutenant in 1852—3 and again in 1858—9. Sculpted by Patrick MacDowell R.A. (1799—1870) and erected in 1866 at a cost of £2,000, it was blown up in 1958.

50

NOS. 18–21 ST STEPHEN'S GREEN were demolished about 1968 to make way for the Stephen Court development. No. 18 had a stucco façade with giant pilasters, remodelled with the addition of a top storey by Nicholas Walsh, cabinet-maker, about 1840. Nos. 19 and 20 had been rebuilt after 1798 but had clearly not stood the test of time. No. 21, with a granite doric portico, was the most imposing of the group and had been built in 1791 by George Maquay on the site of an earlier house. Maquay was a businessman with a sugar-baking concern in Thomas Street and a director of the Bank of Ireland. The earliest recorded occupant of the old house was also a banker, Elnathan Lumm of Castle Street who died in 1708. From 1822, No. 21 was the home for many years of one of Dublin's best known medical families, the Colleses. In this century it was for a time St Andrew's College.

51

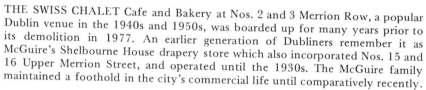

THE SWISS CHALET Cafe and Bakery at Nos. 2 and 3 Merrion Row, a popular Dublin venue in the 1940s and 1950s, was boarded up for many years prior to its demolition in 1977. An earlier generation of Dubliners remember it as McGuire's Shelbourne House drapery store which also incorporated Nos. 15 and 16 Upper Merrion Street, and operated until the 1930s. The McGuire family maintained a foothold in the city's commercial life until comparatively recently.

NO. 15 ELY PLACE was a house of *c.* 1770, substantially remodelled in the Queen Anne style by Sir Thomas Manly Deane (1851–1933) in 1886. He married in 1888 and initially occupied the building solely as a private house. In 1899 he moved in his architectural practice from Upper Merrion Street. Although he contemplated extending over the adjoining laneway and taking in another house the plans came to nothing. In 1908 he sold to Oliver St John Gogarty who lived there until his departure for America in the 1940s. The house and adjoining gardens were purchased by the Royal Hibernian Academy as a site for a new gallery. It was taken down in 1971. The original Academy in Lower Abbey Street, designed and paid for by Francis Johnston, its first President, in 1824, was destroyed in the Rising. The upper portion of the façade was taken down and re-erected in 1929 as the frontage of a business premises built on the site.

IV

FITZWILLIAM TO TARA STREET

The demolition of the sixteen houses NOS. 13–28 LOWER FITZWILLIAM STREET in May 1965 marked the end of a heated debate between the owners, the Electricity Supply Board and their supporters, and the preservationists led by the Irish Georgian Society. The houses were not of great individual architectural importance but were a 400 ft section of Dublin's longest Georgian vista, from Merrion Square to Leeson Street.

Fitzwilliam Street dates from 1792 and these houses were probably later still. Frederick Darley, the architect, lived at No. 25 between 1830 and 1850.

In 1938 the ESB occupied only Nos. 23 and 28 and the two end houses Nos. 29 and 30. Twenty years later, they owned practically the entire east side of the street and had lately erected a substantial office block at the rear. In December 1961 they announced their intention to demolish Nos. 13–28, ending months of speculation about their intentions. It was argued that the buildings were in poor structural condition (evidenced by the numerous steel plates on the façade) and were suffering from dry rot. The parapets had been rebuilt some years earlier. The Board's architectural advisors had requested that an independent opinion be sought from Sir John Summerson as a recognised authority on Georgian architecture. His report on Fitzwilliam Street acknowledged the problem caused by inserting a new building of this magnitude into the area, but questioned the validity of

retaining or reproducing the façades and argued that a neo-Georgian solution would be an historic falsification. Sir John reported that he regarded 'as the only reasonable course' the rebuilding of the houses to 'an entirely new design . . . not necessarily Georgian' in character, which would not conflict 'with their preserved neighbours and yet have positive value of their own'. On his recommendation, the Board decided to hold an architectural competition open to architects in Ireland and Great Britain. The architectural correspondent of the *Irish Times* commented: 'We must heartily

commend the ESB for their determination to approach this truly civic problem in the right way; and hope that their public spirit will be rewarded by the results of the competition.'

The Irish Georgian Society disagreed with the proposal, appealing to the ESB 'to take into account the intense public feeling which would be aroused against them should they proceed with such a very shortsighted scheme', and urging the preservation of what they termed 'the longest, and one of the finest examples of Georgian street architecture in the world'.

53

The Society enlisted the help of another architectural knight, Sir Albert Richardson, who stated that preservation presented no great practical or financial problems. It is intriguing, in view of events later in the decade, that a public meeting at the Mansion House organised by the Irish Georgian Society and the Old Dublin Society was picketed by students of architecture.

The winning scheme, by Stephenson Gibney Associates, was displayed in November 1962. Ministerial planning approval was granted in 1964, and the freehold purchased from Lord Pembroke who donated the proceeds to the IGS. The new building was erected in 1966—70.

In 1906 the government commenced the demolition of most of the west side of UPPER MERRION STREET to make way for the Royal College of Science and what is now known as Government Buildings. Altogether some thirteen houses — the entire block from Leinster Lawn to Lacy's Lane — were taken down, those to the north being the first to go.

According to the Georgian Society Records all these houses were built between 1752 and 1772. By 1756 Nos. 1—3 and 9—13 had been built (1904 numbering).

A survey made six years later shows that a further house, No. 4, had been completed as had some seven houses on the east side. Nos. 5–8 were built as an infill during the following decade, as were the four houses on the south side of Lacy's Lane – Nos. 14–17.

No. 1 (to the extreme right in the photograph) was the largest and probably the oldest of the group, being four bays and 45 ft wide. The doorway of the back drawing-room, of which there is a photograph taken from within the room in the Georgian Society Records, is seen here from the first-floor landing. The walls of the staircase were modelled with plaster panelling in which the panels were raised and the moulding sunk. The door was set in a recess with garlands of flowers upheld by a bird modelled in stuccowork in the tympanum.

The cut limestone entrance doorway of No. 4 was considered by the Georgian Society Records to be perhaps the most interesting in the street. It recalls that built at Newberry Hall, Co. Kildare, attributed to Nathaniel Clements. The stair hall resembled No. 1.

To the right may be seen part of No. 3, a small house which from 1854 to 1861 housed the firm of Deane and Woodward. T. N. Deane continued to practise there until 1899 when it was acquired by the government. He very much regretted leaving, and died shortly afterwards. His son, T. M. Deane, was subsequently appointed executant architect of the new buildings, designed by Sir Aston Webb.

Nos. 5 and 6 were a pair and were, with the exception of No. 1, the largest houses of the group. The Georgian Society Records suggest that they may have been built by Viscount Castlereagh and the Countess of Mayo respectively. The carved stair consoles and door architraves were similar in both houses. The plasterwork of the ceilings of the first floor rooms was similar, but with subtle differences. The same may be said of the stair halls, although No. 6 has some gothic elements. The landing seen in the photograph runs along two walls, while at No. 5 it simply runs from front to back.

On Monday, 13 August 1923, President Cosgrave unveiled a rather curious looking monument on Leinster Lawn. THE CENOTAPH, a temporary structure – plaster on a timber frame, was designed in the form of a stylised Celtic cross by Professor George Atkinson, ARHA, headmaster of the College of Art, and was erected by the Board of Works. In the centre of the cross was the inscription 'Cum Glóire Dé agus Onóra na hÉireann'. It stood in front of Foley's statue of Prince Albert, raised some fifty years earlier (and now moved to one side). Set into the base of the Cenotaph were bronze medallions by Albert Power of Arthur Griffith and Michael Collins. Griffith had died on 12 August 1922, just a year earlier. Ten days after the unveiling of the monument, a wreath-laying ceremony was held to commemorate the first anniversary of Collins' death. Following the assassination of Kevin O'Higgins in 1927, a third plaque was fixed to the plinth. The Cenotaph featured briefly in the news in August 1933 as the proposed venue for a mass parade (banned on its eve) by the supporters of General Eoin O'Duffy, lately dismissed as head of police by President de Valera. It was replaced in 1950 by a 60 ft high granite obelisk, designed by Raymond MacGrath. Medallions of Griffith, Collins and O'Higgins, by Laurence Campbell, were incorporated into its base.

XI.—ANTRIM HOUSE, MERRION-SQUARE,
For years an Hotel.

ANTRIM HOUSE, Merrion Square was built about 1775–8 for the 6th Earl of Antrim to the designs of George Ensor. Following the Earl's death in 1791, the house passed to his daughter, yet was empty in 1798 and was sold several years later. It served for some years as a hotel, then as the residence successively of Robert Shaw MP, Sir Capel Molyneux and Nicholas Leader, Barrister-at-Law, before being divided in half in 1838. The six-bay brick façade was compoed, and the central pedimented doorway was replaced by a window. Flanking doors were inserted on either side. The reception rooms, with their splendid Adam decorations, were distributed between the two houses – Nos. 33 and 34, the hall of the latter being cut off from the front room. The houses, together with the narrow No. 32 at the corner of Holles Street, were demolished in the mid 1930s to make way for the new National Maternity Hospital.

The adjoining houses, NOS. 38 AND 39 HOGAN PLACE, formerly Wentworth Place, on Grand Canal Street were a rare urban exercise in Tudor gothic, probably dating from the 1830s. The style, which is more often seen in the suburbs and country estates, was that favoured by William Vitruvius Morrison (1795—1839), whose father and sometime partner Sir Richard (1767—1849) designed Sir Patrick Dun's Hospital, further along the street, at the turn of the century. The houses were demolished in 1976 to make way for new housing.

The origin of the plaster statue of HIBERNIA, a landmark which stood formerly atop a pier at the junction of Clare Street and South Leinster Street and which disappeared in the late 1950s, is obscure. Wilmot Harrison, writing in 1890, spoke of a Danish wolf dog atop the pier on the other side of the premises — No. 5 South Leinster Street (now Davis King's). He claimed that both had been erected by the patriot Archibald Hamilton Rowan who lived in the house between 1818 and 1826. However, the piers are without statues in the view of the street published in Shaw's Post Office Directory in 1850. It seems more likely that they were erected by the firm of Thomas Panter and Son, painters, gilders and decorators who came here in the 1870s. Curiously, they were still in business when Harrison published his description.

TURKISH BATHS, LINCOLN PLACE were the most architecturally interesting of the Dublin baths. There were others at 11 and 12 Sackville Street Upper, Leinster Street and 127 St Stephen's Green West, the last being the most fashionable. Built in 1859—60, the Lincoln Place Baths were designed by Richard Barter of Cork whose father had patented a Turkish bath system and established at St Ann's, Blarney as one of the leading hydropathical establishments in Europe.

The baths were divided into three sections — male and female with separate entrances in Lincoln Place and 'horses and other animals' with an entrance to Leinster Street. The complex was surmounted by a 50 ft high onion dome behind which rose an 85 ft chimney shaft. The accommodation, which was duplicated with males on the right and females on the left, included divans with platforms above where coffee and chibouk could be had, tepidaria and caldaria. These were 'first and second class arrangements'. The board room, entered via a grand staircase, was situated under the dome. 'The mosque of the baths' was one of Leopold Bloom's first ports of call on 16 June 1904. The establishment had, in fact, closed some five years earlier. After a variety of uses it was finally demolished about 1970.

58

The LINCOLN PLACE ENTRANCE to Trinity College was designed in 1852 by John McCurdy and is his earliest known work. McCurdy, then twenty-nine years old, had lately succeeded his master Frederick Darley as college architect. The inner piers and gates were removed in the mid 1960s to facilitate builders' trucks during the construction of the New Library, but were never reinstated.

The RUBRICS AT TRINITY COLLEGE owe their present appearance to a late nineteenth-century re-modelling during which the ornate gables, roof and chimney stacks were added to the designs of R. J. Stirling. This surviving east range, dating from the early 1700s, was the first of three similar blocks to be constructed around a square which was enclosed on the fourth side with the building of Thomas Burgh's Library in 1712—22.

The photograph shows the north range, demolished in 1901 for Sir Thomas Drew's Graduates Memorial Building. The bow-windowed gable marks the cut made when the west range was taken down in the late 1830s. The west range ran between this point and the north wall of the Library pavilion which it abutted, with a break in the centre occupied by the seventeenth-century chapel (on the site of the present campanile). The chapel had been removed in the 1790s.

QUEEN'S THEATRE, Pearse Street, was opened in 1829 as the Adelphi. In 1844 it was granted a patent as the Queen's Royal Theatre. During the 1880s and 1890s it was run by the English playwright J. W. Whitbread. Remodelled by the architect William Stirling in 1893, it closed again in 1907—9 when it was completely reconstructed to his designs. Although reputedly accoustically perfect, it suffered from a rather tortuous plan. It re-opened in 1909 without the 'Royal' prefix, under the management of Charles F. Wright. It was later operated by Bourke and Wilde, and from 1935 by Paddy Gogan who carried on until 1951 when the Abbey Company moved in. With the opening of the new Abbey in 1966 the Queen's closed down and stood empty until its demolition three years later.

In 1884, MESSRS THOMAS McKENZIE & SONS, agricultural engineers and agents, implement manufacturers, seed, manure and oil cake merchants, moved from Dawson Street to new premises at 212–13 Great Brunswick Street (later Pearse Street), built from the competition winning design of J. J. O'Callaghan. The contractor was James Donovan of Dublin and Dalkey.

McKenzies, built of hard red Irish bricks with Ballyknockan granite dressings, was a typical example of O'Callaghan's 'free Gothic' commercial style though much plainer than his building for Messrs Callaghan in Dame Street and his many hotels and pubs which included the Dolphin (q.v.). The internal structure was of timber supported on cast-iron columns. The building was destroyed by fire in April 1970.

THE WESTMORELAND OR LOCK HOSPITAL (latterly known as the Hospital of St Margaret of Cortona) stood at the junction of Townsend Street and Luke Street until the 1950s. It was built in 1753 as the Hospital for Incurables, in the Palladian style of Richard Castle and his successor, John Ensor, and had a well-proportioned if severe break-front pedimented façade.

When the establishment moved to Donnybrook in 1792 the Townsend Street premises were opened 'for the reception of persons in indigent circumstances afflicted with the venereal complaint'. Several additional wards in the shape of an inverted 'T' were added to the rear.

In 1798 Francis Johnston removed the quadrants which had flanked the main elevation to add a further pair of wards. From 1820 onwards only 'destitute female patients' were admitted, the establishment being supported by parliamentary grants. The pedimented doorcase was salvaged and re-erected by the late John Hunt in his gardens on the Hill of Howth.

TARA STREET was formed in 1885 on the sites of the former George's Street, Shoe Lane and Fleet Market. The photograph, taken about 1930 from the (now disused) Tara Street Baths, shows the west side which predated the name change and which disappeared in further street improvements. These were carried out when the original Butt Bridge, a centre pivoted swing bridge, designed by Bindon Blood Storey (1828–1909) and erected in 1879, was replaced with the present concrete structure by the Dublin Port and Docks Board in 1932, the year of the Eucharistic Congress. In the background may be seen the old Liberty Hall (q.v.) and the Beresford Place premises of Messrs Brooks Thomas which was cleared in the mid 1970s for the Irish Life centre.

V

EAST OF O'CONNELL STREET

The photograph shows the CUSTOM HOUSE by James Gandon (1743–1823) before the view from upstream was obliterated by the Loop Line railway bridge in 1891. In the foreground is the original Butt Bridge (1879), designed to swivel, but in fact only rarely opened to river traffic. To the left of the bridge, at the corner of Beresford Place and Custom House Quay, can be seen Deane and Woodward's obelisk-like drinking fountain (1861) (q.v.).

The skyline of the Custom House itself is rather different from the modern view. It was set on fire by Republican forces on 25 May 1921, during the War of Independence, and completely gutted. In the subsequent rebuilding the chimney stacks were omitted. The four statues over the portico, which were damaged, were taken down and are now preserved in an internal courtyard. Two of these statues were by Edward Smyth (1749–1812). The dome and peristyle were completely rebuilt in Ardbraccan stone rather than the original lighter coloured Portland stone.

(BERESFORD-PLACE.)

(PARKGATE-STREET.)

DRINKING FOUNTAINS IN DUBLIN.
Messrs Deane and Woodward, Architects.

CARLISLE DRINKING FOUNTAINS: George William Frederick Howard, 7th Earl of Carlisle, served as Lord Lieutenant of Ireland during the Palmerston administration of 1855—8. When the Whigs returned to power in 1859 Palmerston had him reinstated and he took up office on 18 June of that year.

That same month he had lectured in England on the subject of drinking fountains, which he supposed could be erected for between £10 and £20 each. At this time a Drinking Fountain Movement was sweeping Britain and many splendid examples were taking shape on the drawing boards of architects and manufacturers alike to satisfy the demands of liberal patrons. The intention was that they would cater for 'a class who, perhaps more than many others of the community usually seek a more exciting beverage than *aqua pura*'. The medieval spirit, if that is the correct word, of the movement was captured in the design by William Burges for a fountain in Gloucester published in *The Builder* in 1858.

Carlisle had promoted a Public Health Bill in 1848 (as Lord Morpeth) and it was not unnatural that the Drinking Fountain Movement should have found him sympathetic to their aims. Shortly after his reappointment as Lord Lieutenant he commissioned Deane and Woodward to design two drinking fountains for Dublin which were subsequently erected at a cost of £50 each.

The fountains were illustrated in an engraving by J. E. Rogers (Woodward's pupil) published in the *Dublin Builder* of 1 February 1861. One was located at the junction of Beresford Place and the quays and was a 10 ft high pillar of limestone and Caen stone on a granite base. Constructed by Purdy and Outhwaite who had worked on the Kildare Street Club, it boasted a charcoal filter and a shelf intended as a 'rest for burdens'. It was demolished in 1891 to make way for the Loop Line. The other 'mural' fountain was set into a wall in Parkgate Street midway between the Viceregal Lodge and the Royal Barracks. Perhaps the *Dublin Builder* had both buildings in mind when it commented that Carlisle's 'characteristic discrimination and truly eminent philanthropy most happily suggested the suitability of this site'. It resembled a Venetian well-head and was located in a recess. Built by Cockburns and carved by Purdy and Company, it has long been blocked up.

In 1864 Carlisle suffered a terminal illness that led to rather genial but eccentric behaviour. Persuaded to retire in October, he died two months later. His statue (q.v.) by J. H. Foley (1818—74) was erected in the Phoenix Park in 1870.

64

THE QUEEN'S MEWS, built around a quadrangle which was entered through an archway in Store Street, was apparently erected early in the nineteenth century as stables for the Custom House. The curvilinear gabled archway within the courtyard, surmounted by a recumbent lion and which survived until the 1950s, probably dated from 1879 when Thomas Drummond Lambert, veterinary surgeon to the Royal Agricultural Society, opened his infirmary and forge here. In the thirty years or so before Lambert restored the Mews to something akin to its original function, it had served as an engineering works and as a bacon-curing establishment. The construction of the Loop Line in 1891 entailed the demolition of the back half of the premises. The archway to Store Street survives as the entrance to a bakery. The rest is gone.

Among the more ambitious commercial buildings projects of the 1820s was NORTHUMBERLAND BUILDINGS at the corner of Eden Quay and Beresford Place. Designed as a hotel and shop development, it later incorporated a Turkish baths with an entrance from Lower Abbey Street. The development never really caught on. After the closure of the Northumberland Hotel and Coffee Rooms, the Beresford Place portion was purchased by the Transport and General Workers' Union as their headquarters in 1912 and was renamed Liberty Hall.

Four years later, bedecked with the banners of Connolly's Citizen Army, it suffered considerable blast damage in the Rising, but was untouched by fire and was subsequently restored. Together with the rest of the Northumberland Buildings it was torn down in the late 1950s to make way for the new Liberty Hall.

THE ABBEY THEATRE opened in 1904 in premises at 27 Lower Abbey Street and 2 Marlborough Street which had once served as the Mechanics' Institute and City Morgue respectively, and which had lately been the Music Hall Theatre. The remodelling was supervised by Joseph Holloway (1861–1944) who had trained under J. J. O'Callaghan, but who is today better remembered for the theatrical reminiscences recorded in his diaries than for any architectural achievements. The auditorium probably incorporated some features dating from John Bourke's (d. 1871) period as architect to the Mechanics' Institute in the 1860s. It was badly damaged by fire on the night of 18 July 1951 and was subsequently demolished. The new Abbey Theatre was opened on a larger site in 1966.

In 1859 the *Dublin Builder* noted that the SACKVILLE PLACE PREMISES of Messrs Dawson & Co., coach builders, had been remodelled for Mr Maurice Brooks, by the architect E. P. Gribbon. The former coachyard was roofed over and floored, creating 'a central apartment larger than an ordinary church'. Messrs Brooks Thomas & Co. continued to trade there until their move to the suburbs in the mid 1970s. An office and shop development now stands on the site.

The designs selected for the PRO-CATHEDRAL in Marlborough Street, as a result of an architectural competition held in 1814, were those sent, we are told, from Paris by the exiled United Irishman, John Sweetman, a member of the Dublin brewing family. His brother William was the competition organiser. The quality of the design, unfortunately modified in execution, does not suggest an amateur, and it is not unlikely that Sweetman obtained the plans from a Parisian architect, possibly Louis Hippolyte Le Bas (1782–1867), whose Notre-Dame-de-Lorette, Paris, designed in 1824 when the Pro-Cathedral was nearing completion, shares several features with the latter.

Notre-Dame-de-Lorette has the clerestory windows of the original Pro-Cathedral design and the dome and apse of the executed design. Both churches have pulpits based on the Athenian choragic monument of Lysicrates. In 1980, the pulpit was moved from the nave and the sanctuary remodelled.

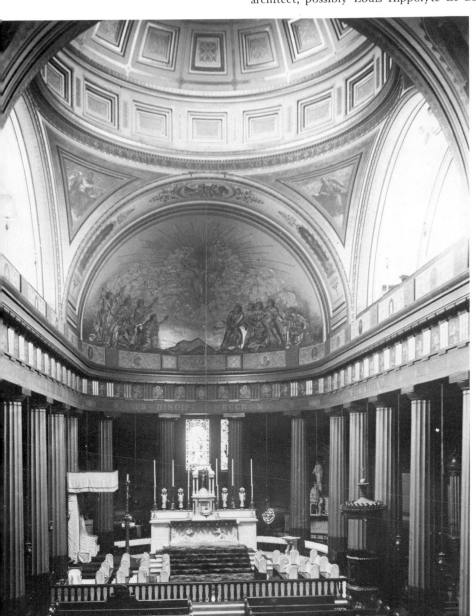

The High Altar, executed about 1823 by the Belfast-born sculptor Peter Turnerelli (1774–1839), was dismantled and its panels rearranged as a base for the tabernacle, which was reduced in height. The panels depict two angels in *bas relief* at either side of a richly carved monstrance. John Gilmartin has noted the similarity between these angels and those of the Tomb of Eugene IV by Isaia de Pisa (*c.* 1450) in S. Salvatore in Lauro in Rome, and between the tomb and the Archbishop Troy Monument in the Pro-Cathedral. Turnerelli also studied the altar in the Duke of Norfolk's private chapel at Arundel Castle in Sussex before making his designs.

67

ST THOMAS'S CHURCH, Marlborough Street, was built in 1758—62 from the designs of John Smyth. Parliament voted three thousand pounds towards its construction. The parish was separated from St Mary's in 1749 and the site chosen for the church on the west side of the street, at the corner of Gregg's Lane, looked out on green fields. With the building of Gloucester Street in the 1770s St Thomas's found itself at the end of a half mile vista. The façade, which was modelled on Palladio's Redentore in Venice, originally had curved sweeps on either side, terminating with pedimented gateways. This gave it a total frontage of 182 feet. However, while Palladio reduced the impact of the nave roof by using a hip, St Thomas's had a rather ungainly gable rising above the portico pediment. The pediment itself was never completed, the cut stone having risen no higher than the architrave.

Many years later Henry Aaron Baker drew up plans for a steeple which would have solved these problems as well as removing the flanking Palladian half-pediments and raising the aisle walls. However, the scheme came to nothing, so that the Venetian St Thomas's came to stand in close proximity with the Parisian Pro-Cathedral down the street. The interior had a flat compartmented ceiling and a gallery supported on corinthian columns. The chancel was decorated with biblical inscriptions in Victorian times by the firm of H. Sibthorpe and Son.

A parochial hall, designed by William Stirling, in what one commentator called 'cement classical' was erected to the north of the church c. 1889.

The church was burnt out in the fire that destroyed much of O'Connell Street in July 1922, when the area was occupied by the Irregulars. Although a contemporary newspaper photograph shows that the façade and main structure survived, an opportunity was taken to extend Gloucester Street (renamed Sean Mac Dermott Street) through to O'Connell Street rather than restore it. In fact there had been a proposal to demolish the church for this reason as far back as 1853 (Moore Street Market q.v.).

A new church in the Byzantine style was designed by Frederick Hicks and erected on the northern side of the new street in 1931—2. Some monuments from old St Thomas's are preserved in the north-west corner.

Among the last surviving houses in Railway Street were Nos. 4, 5 and 6, photographed here in 1951, and occupied during the heyday of MONTO by, respectively, Mrs Lawless, Mrs Hayes and Mrs Quilter. Railway Street was formerly Tyrone Street and before 1887 was Mecklenburgh Street Lower. It was originally called Great Martin's Lane and was renamed for Charlotte Sophia, Princess of Mecklenburgh-Strelitz who married George III in 1761. The later name changes occurred during the era when it was described as 'one of the most dreadful dens of immorality in Europe'.

'Monto' came from Montgomery Street, so named in 1776 for the wife of Luke Gardiner MP. It is now Foley Street. On the west side the 'Digs' or 'Kips', as the place was also known, were bounded by Mabbot Street, now Corporation Street. The eastern boundary was Amiens Street. Some of the houses in Mabbot and Montgomery Streets were owned by the Victorian novelist Charles Lever and his brother Rev. John Lever whose father had built them. According to Dillon Cosgrave, 'The deterioration of this property began in Charles Lever's lifetime and caused him much annoyance'. During the period 1800—1900 it is estimated that Monto was inhabited by some 1,600 prostitutes.

The tenth edition of the *Encyclopaedia Britannica* noted, under prostitution, that 'Dublin furnishes an exception to the usual practice in the United Kingdom. In that city police permit open "houses", confined to one street, but carried on more publicly than even in the south of Europe or Algeria'. While Monto was in fact spread out over several streets, Lower Mecklenburgh Street was the most celebrated.

Among the madames were Mrs Meg Arnott at No. 83, Mrs Meehan at Nos. 86 and 87, and Mrs Annie Mack who operated eight houses on the street. These were the 'flash' houses, and were the setting for 'night-town' in James Joyce's *Ulysses*, where Dedalus and Lynch, following Bloom, knock first at No. 85, one of Mrs Mack's houses, mistaking it for Bella Cohen's establishment at 82. She resided here between 1888 and 1905. Monto went into decline after this date, many of the 'flash' houses becoming ruined and business transferring to the lower numbered houses. Among the survivors listed in the 1924 Thom's Directory were Mrs Meehan at Nos. 85—7, described as 'lodging houses', and Mrs Roberts, alias May Oblong, at Nos. 32—3, to whom reference is made in *Finnegans Wake*. The efforts of the late Frank Duff, which began a year earlier, to rehabilitate the inhabitants resulted in the closure of many brothels. A police raid in March 1925, during which 120 persons, including a country TD, were arrested, effectively marked the end of Monto.

ST BARNABAS' CHURCH, Upper Sheriff Street, begun in 1869, Disestablishment Year, was demolished just a hundred years later. It was designed in the Perpendicular Gothic style by Alfred Gresham Jones, and could seat three hundred. Built as a 'Mariners' Church' at a cost of £4,000, it was one of three churches 'in needy localities' for which a Miss Shannon of Rathmines made provision in her will. The parish schools, also by Jones, were built with £900 donated by James Benjamin Ball JP of Merrion Square.

VI

NORTH AND WEST OF O'CONNELL STREET

MOUNTJOY SQUARE was surveyed and laid out in 1787 as a private undertaking by the Rt Hon. Luke Gardiner MP for Co. Dublin, created Baron Mountjoy in 1789 and Viscount in 1795. An early proposal for the west side which survives shows a unified palatial elevation in the London manner, with central dome, portico and end pavilions. The project by an unnamed architect was stillborn as was a proposal to build a new church for St George's Parish in the centre of the square.

In 1790 the first building leases were granted. Work continued until 1818, by which time 72 houses had been built, 18 on each side. The east side was the last to be completed. The Square, some four acres in extent, was enclosed, planted and laid out with gravel walks by the residents in 1802–3. The landscape gardener John Sutherland (d. 1826) designed the layout. Lord Mountjoy did not live to see the scheme completed. He was killed by a cannonball while leading his regiment at the Battle of New Ross in 1798.

The last of Dublin's squares, Mountjoy, was built during a period of decline: the Act of Union was passed within a few years of its commencement. In 1938 Dublin Corporation took over the Square from the residents who had maintained it since its inception. After the Second World War many of the houses were allowed to deteriorate. Demolition did not begin until the 1960s when Mountjoy Place, which abutted the east side, was taken down. Piecemeal demolition of the south and west sides created ugly gaps in the fabric.

Various efforts were made to rebuild the south side. Preservationist interests, having acquired some of the houses, then endeavoured to find a sympathetic developer to restore them. In the 1970s work began on an ambitious project which involved building a modern block behind and reinstating the Georgian houses in front. Dogged by financial difficulties, work stopped in 1974. The site was sold but building work did not recommence until February 1981. In the intervening period the decline had regrettably accelerated.

NO. 16 MIDDLE GARDINER STREET, built about 1787, survived until the late 1960s when it was taken down to make way for Fr Scully House. It was one of the first houses to be built on Gardiner Street, laid out by Rt Hon. Luke Gardiner. Between 1815 and 1824 it was occupied by Judith Woodward, a grand-aunt of the architect Benjamin Woodward.

No. 16 had an unusual plan: it was double-fronted, five bays wide and only one room deep, the rooms to the left of the central hall having windows to both front and rear. The staircase rose against the back wall on the right-hand side. The fine doorcase was surmounted by an ornate plaster relief. The lights to left and right of it were originally patterned with oval and diamond panes.

From 1943 onwards many houses in this neighbourhood, including sections of Lower Gardiner Street, Sean Mac Dermott Street, Gloucester Place and Summerhill, were reconstructed by the Corporation, new building being greatly restricted by wartime conditions. At the time of writing, most of these houses have been detenanted as part of a redevelopment plan.

The front drawing-room of NO. 41 NORTH GREAT GEORGE'S STREET was claimed, in 1907, to have the only perfect frescoes remaining in the city. While contemporary photographs indicate that some deterioration had taken place, the scenes of the Italian coast seen between the pillars of a loggia were quite discernible. The walls have since been painted over.

According to the Georgian Society Records, the house was built on ground leased in 1786 by Henry Darley, stone-cutter of Abbey Street, from the trustees of the Archdall family, the owners of the lands of Mount Eccles. The frescoes were said to have been carried out by an Italian artist, possibly Gaspare Gabrielli (*fl.* 1805–30), for Sir Richard J. T. Orpen of Ardtully, Kenmare, sometime President of the Incorporated Law Society, who purchased the house before 1819. Gabrielli was brought from Rome by Lord Cloncurry to decorate the dining-room and music-room at Lyons, Co. Kildare.

Isaac Butt MP purchased No. 41 following the death of Orpen in 1876. It later served as Kenmare House Collegiate School and is today a convent. The actual Kenmare House was further down the street at No. 35.

The photograph of NO. 80 LOWER DORSET STREET, which was taken shortly before its demolition in the 1890s, shows a curious scene: an early eighteenth-century mansion with what can be described only as shanties built up against it. It is a scene one might expect in some far-flung outpost of the Empire rather than on the chief artery into the city from the north.

The house was built by Richard Synnot, Register of the Diocese of Armagh, who married Jane Bloxham in 1694. Synnot's father, Thomas, son of a Wexford man and brought up in Derry, settled in Dublin where he attained the office of Town Major. In his will dated 1727, Richard Synnot describes himself as of Drumcondra Lane (as Lower Dorset Street was then known) and late of the city of Dublin.

When it was built the house stood in a rural setting surrounded by market gardens, with the occasional suburban residence fronting onto the road. The doorcase, characteristic of the early eighteenth century, was similar to those at No. 11 Lower Leeson Street and several other Dublin houses illustrated in the Georgian Society Records. The subdivision of the fanlight appears to be similar to that at Platten Hall, Co. Louth (now demolished) c. 1700, attributed to Sir William Robinson (c. 1643–1712). Mouldings, similar to the Synnot doorcase, occurred both at Platten and in the Upper Yard at Dublin Castle — from 1712 onwards (q.v.) — executed by Thomas Burgh (1670–1730) following plans by Robinson. The house was occupied by the Synnot family up to 1789 and probably later. Synnot Place nearby dates from 1795. In 1830 it is mentioned in a marriage settlement between the then resident Dillon O'Connor, land agent, and Frideswida Kellet. A row of Queen Anne style Victorian shops now occupies the site.

HARDWICKE STREET AND PLACE, called after the 3rd Earl who was Lord Lieutenant, were laid out about 1805–7. The vista from North Frederick Street terminates in the crescent-shaped Hardwicke Place and St George's Church, making it what has been termed one of the few architectural set-pieces in the city. The crescent (unlike Bath) never got its companion, the Royal Circus, proposed by Francis Johnston for the far end of Eccles Street. Both the crescent and much of Hardwicke Street itself were demolished by the Corporation for new flat blocks in 1954.

Among the losses in the street was No. 38½, an early eighteenth-century free-standing house probably built by a Major Ferière. It was occupied by the Poor Clares from 1752 until their move to Harold's Cross in 1803. From then until 1816 it served as a chapel of ease, being taken over by the Jesuits in that year and used by them until the completion of their Gardiner Street Church in 1832. They ran a college there for some nine years after this date.

No. 38½ is probably best remembered for its last occupants, the Dun Emer Guild, and for the Mangan Hall, where George Moore and Edward Martyn had their Theatre of Ireland.

NO. 7 ECCLES STREET was one of a row of small three-storey-over-basement houses on the north side near the junction of Dorset Street, demolished in the 1960s. It was remarkable not for its real residents but its fictional ones, Leopold and Molly Bloom in *Ulysses.* Joyce knew the house well, for it was occupied by his friend J. F. Byrne who appears in the novel as Cranly. The front door of No. 7 was salvaged, and has been re-erected in the Bailey in Duke Street.

JOHNSTON'S TOWER: The perpendicular gothic tower to the right of the picture, nestling among the mews houses behind Eccles Street, was erected by the architect and campanologist Francis Johnston who lived at No. 64. The crenellations seen to the left of the belfry were not confined to Johnston's mews. A painting by Henry Kirchhoffer dated 1832 shows that the mews of the adjoining properties were treated to resemble a monastic foundation, giving a very picturesque view from Johnston's windows.

The neighbours were not so keen when Johnston resorted to the tower to sound his peal. The bells were removed to nearby St George's Church (see picture page 73), built to Johnston's designs and completed in 1813. He stipulated the occasions both public and private on which they were to be rung. The Eccles Street belfry, whose plastered exterior had long been neglected, was taken down about 1940.

THE BETHSEDA CHAPEL, Granby Row, was built about 1789 by William Smyth Esq., nephew of Dr Arthur Smyth, Archbishop of Dublin. He later added an asylum for female orphans who were lodged in apartments over the chapel.

In 1794, Rev. John Walker annexed a penitentiary 'for the reception and employment of such women dismissed from the Lock Hospital (q.v.) as wished to return again to the paths of industry and virtue'. They were employed in 'washing, mangling, and plain work'. It was reported that 'no place of worship in Dublin is better attended than Bethesda Chapel, to which the solemnity of the service, the sweet voices of the females, and the excellent purposes for which the establishment was founded, all serve as powerful attractions'.

The institution closed in the early years of this century and the Chapel was acquired by W. M. Shanley Esq. who converted it into the Dorset Street Cinema, opening on 13 May 1913. It was later renamed the Plaza. The adjoining orphan school became tenements and was subsequently demolished. The chapel exterior survived many years of cinema use. In the 1960s the portico was removed and the flanking wall to Dorset Street refaced. The original slate roof may still be seen.

74

Of the sixty-six houses in LOWER DOMINICK STREET in 1938, only twelve survive today. No. 66 at the corner of Parnell Street is the sole survivor at the southern end. Further up, five good eighteenth-century houses remain on the west side — Nos. 39—43 — and a further five on the east — Nos. 20—24. No. 20, built in the 1760s by Robert West and occupied by the Rt Hon. John Beresford, has some of the best rococo plasterwork in Dublin. No. 41, one of the houses still occupied by the Convent of the Holy Faith, was formerly the town house of the Earls of Howth who handed it over to the Carmelite friars in 1800. No. 39, once the residence of Sir William Fownes, has a particularly fine doorcase.

While some houses to the north of the Convent disappeared as recently as 1977, including No. 36, birthplace of the mathematician Rowan Hamilton, most of the demolitions in Dominick Street took place in the late 1950s when the lower east side was cleared, and in the 1960s when the houses opposite were pulled down. These have been replaced by Corporation flats.

Among the disappearances were Nos. 13 and 14, which housed the Leinster Estate Office. Emily Olivia St George, heiress to the estate of her grandfather Sir Christopher Dominick who developed the street in the 1720s, married the second Duke of Leinster in 1775.

The original Dominick residence was among the houses cleared in the late 1850s for the building of ST SAVIOUR'S CHURCH by J. J. McCarthy (1817—82) which has itself undergone significant changes in the past decade, losing its fine Caen stone and marble altar and reredos in the process of modernisation.

75

SEDAN CHAIR RESTHOUSES, PARNELL SQUARE: A detail from Malton's 1793 print of Charlemont House shows the tetra-style Tuscan temple, one of two which stood in the Rotunda Gardens. It was demolished in 1942. The other temple had gone earlier. They both served as rest houses for the sedan-chair carriers. In 1781 there were more private sedan chairs in the then Rutland Square than in any other street or square of the city, a sign of the high status of the residents.

Midway between the two temples on the high ground at the northern edge of the gardens was another structure, a loggia designed by John Ensor and executed by Simon Vierpyl (*c.* 1725—1810), shown on Roque's Map of 1756. The loggia, above a terrace called the Orchestra, sheltered the musicians playing to the fashionable audiences who contributed to the Hospital revenues.

NO. 14 PARNELL SQUARE was built by John Ensor in 1757; he leased it to Arthur James Nevill of Furness, Co. Kildare, the man who had built Tracton House, St Stephen's Green (q.v.), in 1744 and who had in the intervening period lost, through negligence, both his post as Surveyor-General and his seat in parliament. In 1773 Ensor leased the house to Neville's son for the period of three lives. In 1838 it was sold to one John Rutherford.

A number of fine chimney-pieces formerly at No. 14 were illustrated in the Georgian Society Records, as was the fine compartmented ceiling of the back drawing-room. In the front drawing-room was a coved ceiling. Into the painted cove were set four lunette panels depicting Vulcan, Venus, Diana and Mercury, executed by the Dublin artist Jacob Ennis (1728—70). They were based on panels in Pietra da Cortona's Scala di Giove ceiling at the Pitti Palace in Florence. The panels were fortunately saved and removed before the house was vandalised in the late 1970s. The house and No. 13 next to it were demolished in 1980. The panel illustrated here, Diana, is one of three now in the National Gallery.

SIMPSON'S HOSPITAL, PARNELL STREET was built in 1787 by the trustees of George Simpson, a Jervis Street merchant who left his fortune for the founding of an 'asylum for blind and gouty men in reduced circumstances'. The hospital first opened in Putland House on the same site in 1781 and moved to 'Judge Robinson's house' in Jervis Street during rebuilding.

The Putland family were patrons of the cartographer John Roque who paid them the compliment of including the floor plan of their house on his 1756 map of Dublin. Only one other floor plan appeared on the map – that of the Parliament House.

Faced with granite ashlar, Simpson's Hospital had a large entrance hall with two staircases and cost £6,458 to build. Although several architects, among them James Gandon, were consulted about the design, the author is unknown. The craftsmen included Pemberton & Semple, masons, Simon Vierpyl (who may have carved the doorcase) and Charles Thorp, stuccodore. The board room boasted a rather fine marble chimney-piece which cost £140. The principal feature of the mantel was a carved reclining figure. A dining hall was later added at the back of the building.

In 1925, on the removal of the hospital to Wyckham, Dundrum, the building became the offices of Messrs Williams and Woods who erected factory buildings in the former gardens at the rear. It was sold for redevelopment and demolished in 1978.

LANGFORD HOUSE, MARY STREET, like Clonmell House in Harcourt Street and Tyrawley House in Eccles Street, originally stood in its own grounds. It commanded fine views of the Liffey across the fields. Begun after 1697 by Paul Barry, keeper of the Pipe or Great Roll of the Exchequer, it was presumably complete by 1712 when it was sold to Rt Hon. Henry Ingoldsby.

In 1743 it was bought by Rt Hon. H. R. Rowley, father of Viscount Langford, who died in 1796. The house was purchased soon after by the government and used first as a barracks and after 1809 as the offices of the Paving Board who refaced it.

It was acquired in mid-century by Messrs Bewley and Draper, wholesale druggists, and demolished in 1931 to make way for the nurses' home of Jervis Street Hospital. The hall and stair lobbies at the first and second floor levels had entabulatures supported on tuscan columns. The principal interior features were the two first-floor rooms, decorated to the designs of Robert Adam in 1765.

In 1909 James Joyce returned from Trieste and spent some two and a half months in Dublin setting up a cinema at No. 45 Mary Street. The VOLTA, which was backed by a group of Trieste businessmen, opened on 20 December of that year with a showing of Maria Camerini's 'Beatrice Cenci'. The auditorium colour scheme, recalled by the late Lenny Collinge, then an electrical apprentice there, was in crimson and light blue.

Joyce remained in the background, leaving the running of the cinema to Messrs Machnich, Rebez and Novak. The diet of continental films were not to Dubliners' tastes and after a few months the Italians sold out to British Provincial Cinemas who operated it as the Lyceum Picture Theatre.

Up until the late 1940s the skyline of the Henry Street area view from the Pillar was dominated by the 56 ft high copper-domed tower of ARNOTTS, which was flanked by small domes at either end of the façade. Arnotts had been rebuilt, following a fire, in 1894, from the designs of George Palmer Beater (d. 1928).

In 1949 a newspaper piece described the removal of the tower which, it was claimed, 'served no useful purpose. Its design accorded with no known style of architecture, it was utterly useless from a utility point of view, and was always regarded as a piece of misconceived Victorian decoration'. The flanking domes were also removed. To the right of Arnotts in the photograph may be seen the copper dome of Todd Burns (now Penneys) and further right, the dome, surmounted by a flagpole, of the Henry Street Warehouse Company latterly known as Denmark House, Little Denmark Street, an early steel-framed building which was demolished in 1976.

With the clearance of the old markets area between Moore Street and Little Denmark Street by Dublin Corporation in the 1970s, to make way for a major shopping redevelopment, a maze of old streets disappeared. Among them went Cole's Alley, most of Cole's Lane, Horseman's Row, Riddle's Row and Gregg's Lane.

Buildings to the west of Little Denmark Street were also cleared, among them Denmark House, St Saviour's Schools and the Widows Alms House in Parnell Street. All of the west side of Moore Street, to the north of Sampson's Lane (that part which survived the Rising), was taken down.

Moves to redevelop the MOORE STREET MARKET go back as far as 1853 when a Dublin engineer, John S. Sloane (d. 1886) promoted a scheme at the Great Exhibition. He proposed to build lodging houses, baths and a market house, and lay out an arcade between Moore Street and Upper Sackville Street emerging between the Bilton Hotel and the Dorset Institution (q.v.) in Upper Sackville Street. He also proposed the removal of St Thomas's Church, to extend Gloucester Street and to remove Nelson Pillar. The *Irish Builder*, commenting on a revived attempt to promote the project in 1881, thought this last proposal the only good portion in an otherwise 'absurdly utopian scheme'.

The most important element in Sloane's project was the market house which was to be circular like the reconstructed Ormond Market off the quays. He planned to accommodate one hundred victuallers, fishmongers and greengrocers, twice the number previously in the area. The building was to be covered with an iron and glass roof, supported on the external walls, and a central cast-iron column which would also discharge rain-water to cleanse the floor. In answer to the concern in the city at the presence of slaughterhouses in insanitary surroundings, Sloane proposed to accommodate abattoirs around the perimeter of the building. However the financial failure of the South City Markets, opened in 1881, ensured that Sloane never got the backing he desired.

In the early years of the Sweep the thrice-yearly draws were held at the PLAZA, 99–101 Middle Abbey Street, the ballroom being decorated like a set for a Busby Berkeley musical on each occasion—complete with a cast of thousands. The photograph shows the Grand National Draw of 1932.

The Plaza, designed by Donnelly and Moore, was opened in 1928 and offered billiards, dancing, a restaurant and a parking garage in what had previously been the Savoy Billiard Salon, an enterprise that lasted just three years. The site had been redeveloped after the Rising and was occupied for a short period by the Irish Co-operative Clothing Manufacturing Society Ltd. The Plaza was gutted by fire about 1936 and was subsequently taken down to make way for the Adelphi Cinema, designed by the same architect, Robert Donnelly (1878–1948), this time in association with W. R. Glenn of London. The Adelphi opened its doors in 1939.

VII
WEST OF CAPEL STREET AND NORTH WEST SUBURBS

No architect is known for MESSRS McGRATH BROTHERS' tea and sugar stores, No. 3 Bachelor's Walk, demolished in 1978, although the fine romanesque façade was rather reminiscent of W. G. Murray's work. The premises, which extended into Liffey Street and the Lotts, was reconstructed about 1870 for Messrs Robert and James Turbett, merchants, who began trading on the site in the 1850s and sold out to McGraths in 1907.

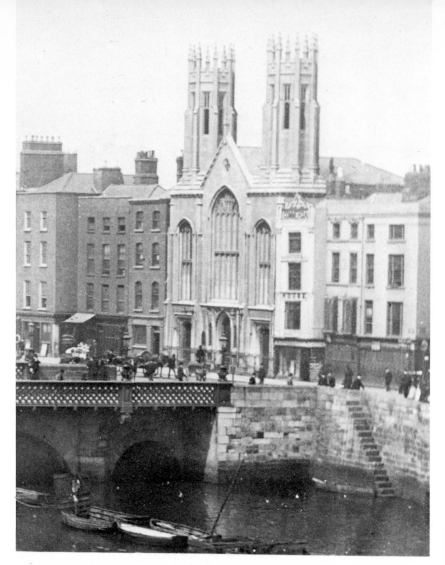

THE PRESBYTERIAN CHURCH, ORMOND QUAY was built in 1846—7 from the designs of E. P. Gribbon who exhibited the drawings at the RHA in the latter year. In 1845 one George Phayre exhibited a scheme for the church suggesting that there may have been a competition. Gribbon's spiky gothic towers, possibly inspired by Hawksmoor's All Souls' College, Oxford, stood out on the quayside skyline.

In 1859, to cater for an increasing congregation, Gribbon was asked to extend and internally alter the building, an exercise which involved the demolition of a schoolhouse at the rear. One hundred years later the church closed and was sold to a developer who proposed a nine-storey office block for the site. However, although all has been demolished with the exception of part of the front elevation, nothing has been built.

In 1932 a number of ornate cast-iron PISSOIRS were imported from France. Most of these were erected along the Liffey quays on the route to the Phoenix Park which was the site of the Eucharistic Congress, held in that year. One of the last of these, on Ormond Quay, long since closed as contravening health regulations, was sold to a student for £10 in the early 1970s. A further example at the junction of Malahide Road and Fairview was still in existence in 1975 but has since been removed.

82

The bronze equestrian statue of GEORGE I by John Van Nost the Elder (d. 1729) was erected on Essex Bridge at a cost of £1,500 and unveiled on 1 August 1722. It was removed to Aungier Street on the rebuilding of the Bridge in 1753. In 1757 a proposal to re-erect it in a projected piazza in front of Dublin Castle in line with Castle Street came to nothing. It was repaired by Van Nost the Younger in the following year.

It was finally moved to the grounds of the Mansion House in 1798 where it was seen by Thackeray who described it as 'peering over a paling near a queer old house'. A proposal of 1815 to re-erect it in Fitzwilliam Square came to nothing. In 1928 it was put up for sale to the highest bidder. No offer materialised until 1937 when it was bought (minus one leg) by the Barber Institute of Birmingham for £100.

On Roque's 1756 map, no houses are shown on the north side of LITTLE BRITAIN STREET. Rather there was a field, probably attached to a large formally planned house to the north which fronted onto Capel Street. Little Britain Street was an extension of Great Britain Street, now Parnell Street, which appears on Brooking's map of 1728. Although this photograph was taken as recently as 1959, apart from the public house to the right, now a café, none of these houses are standing today. Note the wooden shutters on Mrs Mary Quirk's shop, No. 3.

These photographs show two of the interiors of the FOUR COURTS which were destroyed in June 1922 at the height of the Civil War. The plaster figure of Punishment over the central vestibule was one of eight executed between the windows of the inner dome in 1796 by Edward Smyth (1749–1812), sculptor of the riverine heads at James Gandon's other great public building, the Custom House. The other allegorical figures were Justice, Wisdom, Mercy, Liberty, Law, Prudence and Eloquence. In addition there were medallions above each window depicting ancient legislators — Solon, Numa, Moses, Lycurgus, King Alfred, Manco Copac, Confucius and Ollamh Fodhla. The Dublin *Evening Post*, reporting the opening of the Four Courts, noted that, 'The eye [was] particularly attracted by the statue of Punishment who stands on the fasces, the axe surrounded with rods, the strings of which are unbound as letting them loose to execute judgment whilst the statue has its head averted and the hand before the eyes as loth to behold the punishment that justice obliges the law to put into force.'

The second interior illustrated here was that of the double height Law Library, inserted on the first floor of the north east range in 1901. Note the 'palm court' type balconies. This replaced an earlier library in the north-west range and was one of several additions made to the building by the Office of Public Works before 1922.

Neither of these interiors was reproduced in the restoration of the Four Courts, completed in 1932. The plaster decoration on the inner dome is now to a geometric design. A number of statues of modern legislators, which stood in the hall, beneath the dome, were severely damaged in the fire and removed from the debris. They depicted O'Loghlen, O'Hagan, Whiteside, Plunket, Shiel and Joy. Other alterations made in the reconstruction were the removal of chimney-stacks, the shortening of the east and west ranges by some 10 feet, the filling in of the arcades in the north range and the opening of windows in what had previously been niches.

THE FOUR COURTS HOTEL, Inns Quay, began life in 1843 as Samuel Steel's Commercial and Family Hotel. It was soon renamed the Angel. It was damaged by fire in 1864 and reconstructed by the architect E. H. Carson in the following year. During the nineteenth century it passed through several hands, among them Daniel Bergin and Hugh O'Rourke who employed Timothy Hevey (1845–78) to design extensions and alterations, including a new billiard room, in 1869.

In 1902 it was further remodelled and re-opened as the Four Courts Hotel, with Henry Kilbey as manager. In 1938, Kilbey, by now managing director, advertised that the hotel had re-opened following 'reconstruction and refurnishing throughout' and now boasted new tea and smoking lounges, electric elevator and hot and cold running water in each of its hundred bedrooms; 'motor cars for hire and wireless'!

The hotel drew much of its custom from the courts next door. A modern extension was added to the east in the early 1970s, shortly before the hotel finally closed. It remained empty up to 1980 when it was taken down.

NEWGATE GAOL, Green Street, was opened in 1781 and replaced the gaol in the Old Castle tower on the town wall over the gate leading from Cutpurse Row to Thomas Street. The foundation stone of Newgate was laid in 1773. Two years later Thomas Cooley was appointed architect.

While elevational details recall George Dance's London Newgate begun in 1770, Cooley's design was quite different in plan, with four circular towers, one at each corner of a rectangle 170 ft by 130 ft. Individual cells, of which there were ninety-seven, measured 12 ft by 8 ft. There were two yards, a chapel and an infirmary. The location of the latter rooms was criticised by Pool and Cash as were the narrow staircases. The gaol was opened in 1781 and cost £16,000, some £6,000 more than the original estimate. The construction proved to be defective; within four years the mortar was found to be crumbling and by 1787 it was in such a bad state as to be termed 'a malstructure of a prison'. Nevertheless, it remained in use up to about 1860, latterly housing female prisoners. A proposal to demolish and replace it with a new market (q.v.), designed by E. H. Carson in 1869, came to nothing. Instead, the gaol walls were reduced to single storey height, pedimented gateways were inserted and conical roofs fitted to the corner towers. In this condition it served as a fruit market up to the early 1880s. The remaining portions were taken down in February 1899. The bases of the walls mark the boundary of the present St Michan's Park.

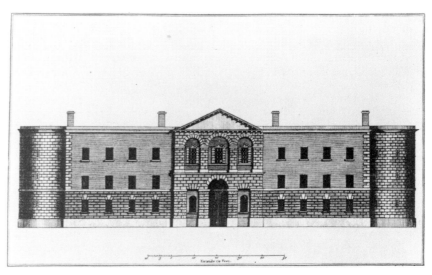

Few Dublin public buildings have had such a chequered history as the LINEN HALL, seen here in Brooking's engraving made in the year of its erection, 1728. The first meeting of the Board of Linen Manufacture was held at Dublin Castle on 10 October 1711 pursuant to an Act of Parliament. Seventy-four trustees were appointed, spread almost equally between the four provinces (Leinster had twenty, the others eighteen). The meetings continued to be held at the Castle until 1716 when a room in Cork Hill was taken.

In 1722 it was decided to build a Linen Hall funded by the Government to cater for a substantial increase in trade. Various sites were offered. That chosen, off North King Street, was acquired for £360 from a Mr Everard who held it from Thomas Pooley. In August 1722 James Byrne was appointed overseer of the building of the Hall, which took the form of a square block with a central courtyard.

The pedimented front faced south along the axis of North Anne Street and George's Hill. The building was surrounded by a walled yard with gates in the centre of each of the four sides and flanking lodges at either end of the front wall. The Hall was opened to traders on 14 November 1728. The board-room was not initially in the hall but in a nearby house.

While Brooking's engraving shows chimney stacks, in the nineteenth century at any rate no light or fire of any kind was permitted, business being confined to the hours nine to five. Among the officials appointed was a night watchman to call 'each hour outside the porter's lodge'.

Roque's Map of 1756 shows that further buildings had been added along the northern, western and eastern walls, facing onto Derry, Coleraine and Lurgan Streets respectively. The entrance front was on Lisburn Street. The names indicate the strong position of the northern linen industry. Roque also shows a flax manufactory nearby, and to the north-east the new Yarn Hall.

Between 1700 and 1775 exports of linen rose from four hundred to sixteen hundred tons. During that period the Irish Parliament granted more than £1¼ million to the industry. By 1775 too, three-quarters of the linen exported was being manufactured in Ulster. Linen in its various shapes and forms was brought to Dublin and stored at the Hall.

In 1781, Derry Street was closed to make way for further additions designed by Thomas Cooley (1740—84) assisted by Francis Johnston. The courtyard of the old Hall was filled in and a bell tower and clock fitted above the main front about this time. The Yarn Hall was also greatly extended with the formation of a second quadrangle while further ranges linked the two Halls into one complex covering nearly three acres. Altogether there were six large courts, with piazzas at ground level and galleries above. In 1821 it was reported that 'the linen-hall contains 557 rooms, occupied by 36 factors, and 130 country drapers, an elegant coffee-room, and a board-room for the trustees'. Of the total, 492 rooms were 'appropriated to the storage of linens, and the remainder to yarns'.

King George IV paid a visit to the Hall on 23 August 1821. A marble statue of the monarch by Thomas Kirk was subsequently erected by the merchants in the corridor of the Hall. After the Act of Union, competition from cotton and the British coarse linen industry adversely affected the situation in Ireland. The Ulster linen industry, accounting for the bulk of production, became industrialised. Some manufacturers were licensed to seal their own packages for export, lessening the work of the linen halls. Ulster had got its own hall in 1783. In 1827 the Parliamentary grant was reduced and in the following year discontinued. The Linen Board was abolished and the halls vested in the Lord Lieutenant. Business at the Dublin Linen Hall was greatly reduced. Thackeray wrote in 1843 in his *Irish Sketch Book:* 'I need not say how we went to see the Linen Hall of Dublin, that huge, useless, lonely, decayed place in the vast solitude of which stands the simpering statue of George IV pointing to some bales of shirting, over which he is supposed to extend his august protection.'

By 1851 the northern part of the building was occupied by the army as a 'temporary barracks'. By 1867 the Factors of the Linen Hall had handed over the remainder to the military authorities. The Yarn Hall, separated from the barracks by a new wall running across courtyards and corridors from north to south, was then sold to Messrs Hugh Moore and Alexander, wholesale druggists who had previously operated in Capel Street.

THE SMITHFIELD PENITEN-
TIARY was opened in 1805 by the
Lord Lieutenant, the 3rd Earl of
Hardwicke. Built to accommodate
female prisoners, by the 1830s it
had been converted to house juvenile
convicts (i.e. aged nineteen and
under). Lewis noted in 1837 that
all prisoners were regularly employed. It next became a convict
depot and served in this role until
1870.

In the following year it was in
use as an R.I.C. depot but remained
unoccupied during 1872 and 1873
before being adopted temporarily
as a branch of the North Dublin
Union. By 1876 it was again vacant,
and judging from the photograph
seems to have become stables with
hay lofts in the upper cells. (Smithfield was the venue for Dublin's hay
market until quite recently.) The
view looks north into the upper
yard. There was a further cell block
to the south. The top of a Smithfield house can be seen over the
roof to the left. The site was
cleared for housing in the 1970s.

By the end of the nineteenth century the army presence at the Linen Hall
seems to have been purely in a caretaking capacity. In 1902 there were proposals
to move some of the paupers from the North Dublin Union into it. Nothing
further happened until 1914 when it was the venue for the Dublin Civic Exhibition.

Hopes of permanent rehabilitation receded with the outbreak of war and the
installation of the Army Pay Department. The building was attacked in the
Rebellion and extensively damaged by fire. The flames spread to Hugh Moore
and Alexander's, destroying all but the gateway to Yarn Hall Street (attributed
to Cooley) and the adjoining range of offices. They subsequently rebuilt the
premises as a polish factory, retaining some of the old walls.

The buildings were acquired by the City of Dublin Vocational Education
Committee in the 1960s and modernised and extended as a technical college.
Although known as the Linen Hall, strictly speaking it is the Yarn Hall. The
ruins of the Linen Hall proper were demolished after the First World War. A
Corporation housing scheme was built on the site.

BLACKHALL STREET was laid out about 1789 on the site of Oxmantown
Green, formerly occupied by 'The Hospital and Free School of King Charles the
Second' or Blue-Coat School. This had been torn down in 1783 on completion
of Thomas Ivory's new school building further to the west. Ivory (c. 1732—86)
had furnished plans for building lots on the new street, intended as a suitable
approach to his elaborate project. However, he resigned in 1780 when asked by
the building committee to make reductions in the school design.

The chairman of the committee, Sir Thomas Blackhall, for whom the street
was named, had been Lord Mayor in 1769. The Corporation, to whom the
charter for the school had been granted in 1671, and the board of governors
granted building leases for 20 ft wide plots. The south-east end was built first,
much of it by Thomas Wildridge of Harcourt Street, and was the only section
to have been completed when Faden published his map of Dublin in 1797. The
section opposite it on the corner of Queen Street is seen here in decayed condition in the 1960s. At the time of writing all had been demolished, with the
exception of two dilapidated houses on the south side.

87

BECTIVE HOUSE was erected on the north-west side of Smithfield in 1738–9 by Sir Thomas Taylour, afterwards 1st Lord Headfort and Earl of Bective. The design, by Richard Castle, included extensive stables running back to Queen Street.

The Queen Street façade — two storeys with a large archway flanked by round-headed windows with granite quoins, and the end portions of the rustication on the entrance front — are all that survive. The Earl's arms are said to have been placed above the hall door, although this is not apparent from the engraving illustrated here. According to one account, Taylour's choice of site away from the fashionable domestic areas, was influenced by commercial considerations — he had made a large sum of money as a grazier and desired to superintend his sales in person.

The family moved their Dublin residence to Rutland (Parnell) Square in 1790. This house, formerly occupied by a son of Archbishop Cobbe, was occupied only briefly by Bective, who died in 1794. It was sold after the Union and demolished in 1863 to make way for Findlater's Church.

Meanwhile the Smithfield house was converted by Robert L'Estrange into a farming-implement factory when he moved his business from the North Wall in 1816. The house was demolished by the firm some time before 1867.

BRUNSWICK VILLAS, off North Great Brunswick Street, photographed here in 1947, had the appearance of a village grouped around a green with a pump at its centre. According to Flora Mitchell, this was a coaching stop on the ancient thoroughfare to Dublin, although Roque's Map (1756) shows only fields here behind the houses on Channel Row, renamed Brunswick Street in the following decade.

FOSTER AQUEDUCT, BROAD-STONE was constructed about 1800 by the Royal Canal Company as a link to the canal harbour across the junction of Phibsborough Road and Constitution Hill. Designed by Millar and Ruddery, architects, it consisted of a single 30 ft span, 15 feet in height flanked by two smaller arched passages for pedestrians. It was dedicated to John Foster, Baron Oriel, late speaker of the Irish Parliament. A stone plaque bore the inscription 'serus in coelum redeas, dique, populo Hiberniae intersis'.

In 1878–9 the Midland Great Western Railway, who had bought the canal in 1845, built a new vehicular approach to the Broadstone station and capped the aqueduct with an iron superstructure by Messrs Courtney and Stephens, converting it to a road bridge. Demolition was first mooted in 1939 but postponed until 1951 when the aqueduct was removed to ease a traffic bottleneck. The plaque unfortunately broke up during at attempt at salvage.

THE FEMALE ORPHAN HOUSE (latterly Kirwan House) on the North Circular Road was opened initially at No. 42 Prussia Street for five orphans by Mrs Edward Tighe and a Mrs Este in 1790. In the following year they were succeeded by Mrs Peter La Touche who commissioned the architect Whitmore Davis to design a new building on the North Circular Road, completed in 1793. In 1796 a west wing was added with the £1,015, raised by a sermon preached by the celebrated orator and former Jesuit, Rev. W. B. Kirwan, in St Peter's. In 1818–19 an east wing and chapel were added to the designs of William Farrell (d. 1853).

The chapel interior with its soaring Gothic vaulting was strongly influenced by the Dublin Castle Chapel Royal, whose architect, Francis Johnston, may have been Farrell's master. There was accommodation for 160 children in the institution. In the late 1960s the buildings were demolished to make way for a hotel which was partly constructed and then sold and completed as an office block.

89

THE MAIN ENTRANCE TO THE PHOENIX PARK, at the junction of Parkgate Street and Conyngham Road, consisted of four circular limestone piers capped by gas-pumps flanking the three vehicular gates with pedestrian gates in the flank walls. While the enclosure of the Park dates from the seventeenth century, these gates were relatively modern, being Victorian. Roque's Map (1756) shows gates at approximately the same point with a lodge to the left, on the site of that in the photograph. The gates were removed for the Eucharistic Congress in 1932, after which it was decided not to reinstate them.

CARLISLE STATUE: The bronze statue of William Frederick Howard, 7th Earl of Carlisle was unveiled in the People's Garden in the Phoenix Park on 2 May 1870. The sculptor was John Henry Foley, who also did the O'Connell Monument. It was cast by H. Prince & Co. of Southwark. Carlisle had first come to Ireland as chief secretary in 1836—41 and served as Lord Lieutenant in 1855—8 and 1859—64. The statue was blown up in July 1958 and landed on its feet with relatively little damage. It was dispatched to the Royal Hospital. The pedestal survives *in situ*.

GOUGH MONUMENT: Dublin's last equestrian statue was unveiled in February 1880 in the Phoenix Park and bore the following inscription on its base: 'In honour of Field-Marshal Hugh Viscount Gough K.P., G.C.B., G.C.S.I., an illustrious Irishman, whose achievements in the Peninsular War, in China, and in India, have added lustre to the military glory of this country, which he faithfully served for seventy-five years. This statue (cast from cannon taken by the troops under his command and granted by Parliament for the purpose) is erected by his friends and comrades.'

The erection of a Gough memorial, first proposed in 1869, was hindered by the failure of the committee to find a suitable site — Carlisle Bridge, Foster Place and Westmoreland Street being vetoed in turn by the Corporation. The commission was given to J. H. Foley and completed after his death in 1874 by Brock Birch and Dewick. A shortage of funds meant that the horse was made from a cast used by Foley for a statue of Lord Viscount Hardinge, one time Governor General of India, in 1857. On the morning of Christmas Eve 1944 the head of the rider was cut off and the sword removed from its hand. The head was later discovered in the Liffey at Kingsbridge. In November 1956 the right hind leg of the charger was blown off. Finally on 23 July 1957 a massive explosion hurled the statue from its base. The remains were removed to the Royal Hospital.

ELEPHANT HOUSE OR 'ALBERT TOWER', Zoological Gardens, was erected in 1845—6 to the designs of George Wilkinson (1813/14—90) at a cost of £370.17.6. Originally built for Albert, a giraffe acquired from London Zoo in 1844, it also contained quarters for an elephant and a camel, and doubled as an observation tower. Following Albert's death in 1849 it became an elephant house and remained in use until the late 1950s. The wall vents were not unlike those at Wilkinson's Harcourt Street Station. Part of the fabric survives within the structure of the present hippo house.

THE SCHOOL HOUSE, GLAS-NEVIN, was built, it was said, in the shape of an ink bottle at the suggestion of Dean Swift. It was demolished in 1901.

DELVILLE, Glasnevin, got its name from Dr Patrick Delany, Fellow and Chancellor of Trinity College Dublin, sometime Chancellor of St Patrick's, Rector of St Werburgh's and friend of Swift. In 1719 he rented a house on the site, called the Glen, with another TCD Fellow, Dr Richard Helsham, and renamed it Heldelville. Delaney subsequently became the sole tenant, truncated the name and partly demolished it to build a new house. The late C. P. Curran suggested that this took place before 1729.

In 1741 Delany's wife died, leaving him an income of £1,000 per annum. Two years later he married the remarkable letter-writer and artist Mary Granville. Born near Devizes in 1700, she had married at the age of eighteen Alexander Pendarves of Cornwall, a man over forty years her senior. Widowed six years later, she first visited Dublin in 1731 when she danced in the Castle ballroom (q.v.), fitted up by Sir Edward Lovett Pearce (c. 1699–1733). Twelve years later she returned to marry Delany. By the time she became mistress of Delville the gardens were already mature. Dr Delany was a friend of Alexander Pope and had returned from visits to Twickenham in the 1720s with all the latest ideas in garden design.

Among the structures he erected in the grounds was a temple with the motto 'Fastigia Despicit Urbis' written on the entablature, a punning reference, supposedly penned by Swift, to Delville's elevated position. Mrs Delany later wrote that 'as we sit by the fireside we can see the ships ride in the harbour', and indeed she illustrated the scene in one of her many drawings of the gardens. The temple, which seems to have been built largely of lath and plaster, had a cellar where Swift reputedly printed his broadsheets. On one wall was a fresco painting of St Paul and into another was set a medallion bust of Stella. Of the house itself we have an excellent description by Mrs Delany.

In the photograph, the earlier wing can be seen to the right of the main house with its breakfront gable wall. The room beneath the bay window (a later insertion) was the eating parlour 'large enough for two sideboards'. The corresponding room on the left of the entrance hall was 'designed for a chapel' which, she commented, they would finish 'as we ought to do . . . when we are rich enough'. She herself completed the decoration with shells. A detail of the elaborate shell-work cornice simulating floral arrangements is reproduced by Curran who also gives a full description of the various rooms: several had fine plasterwork.

Following Dr Delany's death in 1768, his widow removed to England where she continued her handicrafts, most notably her celebrated flower collages, into her eighties; she died in 1788. Wilmot Harrison noted that nineteenth-century owners of the house (among them Sir Patrick Keenan) were conscious of its merits and maintained some of the rooms in their original condition. In fact the decoration survived largely intact, to be destroyed totally when Delville and its temple were pulled down in 1951.

VIII

SOUTH WEST CITY AND THE LIBERTIES

RICHMOND BARRACKS, Inchicore, one of a number of Dublin buildings named after Charles Lennox, 4th Duke of Richmond, was built in 1807, the year of his appointment to the office of Lord Lieutenant. East and west courts were divided by a 300 yard long range with a central portal surmounted by a cupola. In 1831 the Barracks accommodated 'almost 2,000 souls'. Later in the century additional buildings were erected in the east court parallel to the main range.

In December 1922 the Barracks was handed over to the Free State army. In the following year it was renamed Keogh Barracks after Commandant General Tom Keogh, and in 1925 it was converted to housing — a purpose for which it was particularly unsuited. By the late 1960s Keogh Square, as it was known, was regarded as one of 'the city's greatest blemishes'. In 1968 most of the site was cleared and redeveloped as St Michael's Estate.

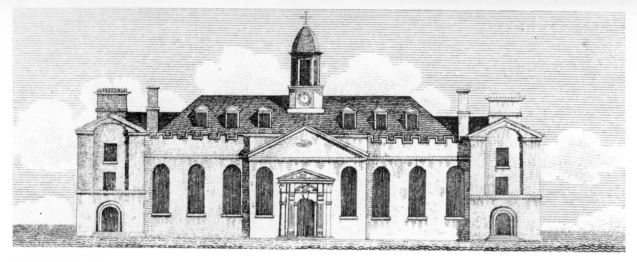

FOUNDLING HOSPITAL: The foundation stone of the Foundling Hospital, James's Street, was laid by the Duchess of Ormonde in 1703 on land acquired by the Corporation. It originally served as a workhouse for the reception of beggars, but by 1725 half the inmates were children taken in off the streets. It was converted to cater for foundlings in 1730.

The principal feature of the building was the dining-hall (capable of accommodating 1,200 children), possibly by Richard Mills, assistant to the Masters of the city works, which had lofty windows rising to the vaulted plaster ceiling and creating an effect which Dr Craig has likened to that of a Wren church which has lost its galleries. In about 1798 Francis Johnston added wings, a crenellated parapet and a cupola. Further work was carried out to the cupola, which incorporated a clock, by Johnston's successor, William George Murray, in 1861.

Murray may also have been responsible for the gothic revival Protestant chapel, the addition of which caused the removal of the handsome pedimented doorway. In 1839 the establishment had reverted to its original role of workhouse — as the South Dublin Union. The existing Foundling chapel, also by Johnston, was converted for Catholic use. Much of the old hospital including both chapels and the dining-hall have been swept away, the latter in about 1957.

THE CITY BASIN, Basin Lane, was constructed by the Corporation in 1721—22 as a reservoir for the cisterns at St James's Gate; the supply was taken from the Poddle River at Dolphin's Barn Mill. The site chosen for the Basin consisted of three fields in the grounds of the Workhouse (q.v.) from where it was reckoned the best fall could be gained.

The Surveyor General, Captain Thomas Burgh, was consulted about the design, which called for a storage capacity of five million hogsheads of water, enough to supply the city for fifty to sixty days. The work was entrusted to James Nelson, assistant to the Masters of the City Works, who claimed £60 for his troubles stating that he had suffered 'great fatigue in bringing a leaden main from the said Bason to James's Street'.

The city gardener, Robert Moody, was responsible for landscaping the borders between the Basin and the surrounding wall which was half an English mile in circumference. The tree-lined gravel walk became 'one of the most fashionable promenades in the vicinity of Dublin'. Concerts were held regularly and there was the occasional fireworks display.

Making the City Basin exhausted the coffers of the Corporation and necessitated a loan of £1,000, borrowed at 6 per cent. Captain Burgh was presented with a piece of plate, 'not exceeding in value £50', for his advice on this and other city projects, among them the erection of the George I statue (q.v.).

Two further basins at Blessington Street and Portobello were erected later in the century. The city's wooden conduits were replaced by metal pipes in 1802. The supply to James's Street City Basin was terminated on 24 June 1869 following the completion of the Vartry Water Works, while Portobello was closed in 1870.

The elegant gateway of the City Basin, seen here much as it was in Brooking's illustration of 1728, survived *in situ* up until 1963 when it was removed to Leixlip Castle, Co. Kildare. The metalwork may be partly original but is stamped with the name of a mid nineteenth-century ironfounder, Murphy of Church Street. Corporation flats now stand on the Basin site.

VICTORIA WHARF was built alongside Victoria Quay in 1873 by Arthur Guinness, Son and Co., to berth the barges that transported the export porter from the nearby brewery downstream to the port of Dublin. Because of the restricted height under the Liffey bridges, the barges had hinged smokestacks. Painted in the company's blue and cream livery, with red and black funnels, the Killiney, Sandyford, Chapelizod and their sisters were a familiar sight on the river until July 1961 when they were replaced by road transport. Four were sold to Robert Scott and Sons of Toomebridge, Co. Antrim, for transporting sand and gravel across Lough Neagh, while a fifth went to Haulbowline, Co. Cork.

JAMES'S STREET HARBOUR was completed by the Grand Canal Company in 1785. It originally comprised two rectangular basins and was subsequently extended with the addition of a semi-circular inner basin to the north, and a further harbour to the east, separated by a drawbridge.

The latter was the private venture of Sir James Bond, who leased the ground from the company in 1786 with the idea of setting up a market in buildings erected around the harbour. The venture was not a success and the markets were abandoned in 1817.

In 1858 the drawbridge was replaced with a new structure nicknamed the 'Rupee Bridge' after the lessee, Bond's descendant Colonel Hutchinson, who resided in India.

Bond Harbour was acquired by Guinness's who filled in the northern half in 1885–6 to build the Malt Store, which incorporated a wharf for unloading malt sacks from barges. In 1863 the Grand Canal Company moved their head offices to James's Street Harbour from South William Street. From the middle of the nineteenth century, the canals suffered increasing competition from the railways. During the last war they enjoyed a brief recovery, which was not sustained with the return of road transport after 1945. In 1950 the Grand Canal Company merged with Córas Iompair Éireann.

The last boats to operate commercially on the canal were those carrying stout to Limerick from James's Street Harbour which continued up until May 1960, some months after other traffic had ceased. The last bargeload of malt had been discharged at the former Bond harbour about a year earlier.

In 1960 the middle and inner harbours were filled in, while further storage facilities were erected on the site of the malt house harbour. In 1978 the Corporation filled in the remainder as well as the connecting stretch of canal back to the first lock to create a linear park. The Canal Company offices have been demolished. The fine semi-circular store (pre-1866) at the top of the inner harbour, which was once an experimental maltings, survives as a furniture warehouse.

A 1940s account of this curious house (since demolished) in OLD KILMAINHAM speculated that the then lately revealed statue over the doorcase, previously hidden by ivy, was that of William Shakespeare, but offered no clue as to its origin. The house was reputedly that of a miller and appears to have been re-roofed in the nineteenth century. The arrangement of the windows on the upper floor would suggest that it was originally gabled.

96

MOIRA HOUSE, Usher's Island, was built in 1752 by John Rawdon, 1st Earl of Moira. Only one view, William Brocas Junior's engraving of 1811, is known of its original form. The doll's house appearance, with centre pedimented breakfront and wide modillion cornice, belie its late date. Like Powerscourt House built twenty years later, it was flanked by pedimented archways. Among the internal features was an octagonal room, 20 ft across and 15 ft high, admired by John Wesley on a visit in 1775.

The Dowager Lady Moira was sympathetic to the nationalist cause and Emmet is said to have used the house. She died in 1803, the year of Emmet's rising. The house was sold by her son George Augustus, the 2nd Earl of Moira, Marquess of Hastings, Earl of Rawdon and Viscount Loudon, who had extensive estates in England and Scotland. It was acquired in 1826 by the 'Association for the Suppression of Mendicancy in Dublin', who spent £7,825, part of a legacy, on its purchase and reconstruction as the Mendicity Asylum.

The remodelling appears to have involved doubling the house in width, probably by extending it to the east. The pediment, modillion cornice and top storey were removed and a new balustrade erected. The entrance was re-centred on the new façade.

The Mendicity Institution, as it is best known, was founded in 1818 'to repress as far as possible obtrusive street beggary and to relieve pressing casual want in our city', and had its first home in the former Royal Dublin Society premises in Hawkins Street. This proved too far removed from the centres of poverty, necessitating a move to Copper Alley, off Fishamble Street, in 1821 from where they went to Moira House.

Moira House was occupied by Sean Heuston and a group of about twenty-five Volunteers during Easter Week 1916 and was badly damaged in the ensuing siege. It was repaired and continued to serve the Institution up until 1954. It was demolished in the 1960s.

On Saturday, 8 May 1877, the Viceroy, the Duke of Marlborough, opened the new front wing of the COOMBE LYING-IN HOSPITAL, begun two years earlier from the designs of J. F. Fuller (1835—1924), favourite architect of the hospital's main benefactors, the Guinness family, who had previously built a dispensary wing. At the time, Fuller was engaged on two large commissions for Sir Arthur Guinness (later Lord Ardilaun): the extension of St Anne's, Clontarf, (q.v.) and Ashford Castle, Cong. He replaced D. C. Ferguson as the hospital's architect.

The new wing, an exercise in sombre neo-Georgian, consisted of offices at first-floor level and wards on the upper floors, which increased the number of beds from thirty-one to seventy. The hospital had been founded in 1826 by Mrs Margaret Boyle, a wealthy widow, prompted by the death in Thomas Street of a woman unable to reach the Rotunda, then the only lying-in hospital in the city.

Mrs Boyle took over the old Meath Hospital on the Coombe, built in 1770—73 and vacated in 1822 on the completion of the new Meath Hospital in Long Lane. In the 1960s the Coombe Hospital removed to a new complex on Cork Street. Part of the old building was used for a time as a Red Cross day-centre for the elderly and needy of the area. All that survives now of the old hospital is the Fuller portico from the Coombe which Dublin Corporation have incorporated into a new housing development.

HOME'S HOTEL, Usher's Quay: George Home, a Scotsman, revolutionised Dublin shopping with the erection of the Royal Arcade, linking Suffolk Street and College Green in 1819 and built at a cost of £16,000. In 1826 he spent a further £20,000 on a large two-hundred-roomed hotel and cloth market, the Wellesley Market at Usher's Quay.

The Royal Arcade was destroyed by fire in 1837 while the hotel passed into the hands of a sect known as the White Quakers who established a weaving manufactory there. By 1878 Nos. 18, 19 and 20 Usher's Quay had become the premises of James Ganly, auctioneer, salesmaster, corn and wool broker, and house agent. When Ganly's moved to new premises on Usher's Island in 1977 the old hotel was demolished. The septastyle doric portico which featured in the old engravings had been taken down many years earlier.

THE MARSHALSEA BARRACKS, off Bonham and Bridgefoot Streets, was built in the 1770s as the Four Courts Marshalsea, replacing an earlier building of the same name behind Wood Quay. Some sources place its construction in the 1740s. The Annals of Dublin, however, state that the foundation stone was laid in 1775.

In the Marshalsea debtors were confined from all parts of Ireland with their wives and families. The buildings were ranged around an upper court which housed the Marshal and his deputy, the tap, guard room, common hall and prisoners' rooms. In the lower court were the chapel, infirmary, ball court, common bath and privies. Despite the construction of additional accommodation in the early nineteenth century, the Marshalsea was described in 1821 as extremely overcrowded, while the confined site impeded ventilation. Most prisoners had to pay rent (exorbitant in the early days), while the poorer inmates, although rent free, were supplied with bread only in cases of extreme indigence.

During the latter half of the nineteenth century, the Marshalsea served as the barracks of the Dublin company of militia. After the Rising, British troops were quartered there. Later it accommodated 'drop out' tenants from other Corporation housing, serving in this role until 1970. It stood empty for some years before being demolished, some of the stone going to repair the city wall at Cook Street in 1975.

With the widening of Bridge Street in the late 1970s as part of the inner tangent road scheme, a number of houses (Nos. 4—9) in CORNMARKET disappeared. Beyond them may be seen Purcell's Alley leading down to St Audeon's Arch. Unfortunately in the twenty years or so since this photograph was taken the terracotta piers and railings erected alongside the alley in the late nineteenth century have been subjected to much abuse. The Winstanley Memorial Hall, later the premises of Harwood Bros. Ltd, was built for the parish of St Audeon in 1894—6 from the competition-winning designs of William Stirling. It was demolished in 1980.

The photograph shows a panelled first floor room in NO. 36 BRIDE STREET, occupied in the eighteenth century by George Dowdall, a solicitor in the Court of the Exchequer, but believed to date from the late Stuart period. It was built some time after 1666 on the west side of the street on the former gardens of the Treasurer of St Patrick's Cathedral.

The Georgian Society Records published photographs and measured drawings of the interior. There was also a fine staircase and a wainscotted lobby. They described the interiors as 'quite unlike any other work in Dublin'. The ground floor had been altered in the eighteenth century, possibly in 1771, when a chemist and druggist, coincidentally named Patrick Bride, took the premises. The front elevation, five bays wide, was thought to have been rebuilt at this time, when what was probably a gabled profile was replaced by a flat parapet. The house was occupied by a succession of wholesale chemists and druggists up until 1909. It was subsequently divided into tenements. Demolished in 1963, it appears in a view published by Flora Mitchell in *Vanishing Dublin*.

In the late 1890s and early 1900s the vast warren of streets between St Patrick's Cathedral and the back of Christchurch Place was cleared to make a new park and build a model housing development funded by the Guinness family — the Iveagh Trust Buildings. The area known as BULL ALLEY was regarded as one of the worst slums in the city. The photograph, one of several taken in the vicinity for Lawrence before its clearance, shows buildings on the site of St Patrick's Park looking towards Patrick Street, venue of a famous street market.

CHAPTER PLACE or Lane, formerly known as Mitre Alley and Deanery Lane, was laid out on the grounds of the Vicar's Choral between St Patrick's Close and Kevin Street. The house on the left, opposite the Cathedral and fronting onto St Patrick's Close, is thought to be related stylistically to the curvilinear-gabled houses on Sweeny's Lane, dating from 1721 (q.v.). Note the whitewashed walls in the foreground and the drain running down the middle of the street.

The site is now part of the Cathedral choir school.

THE WEAVERS HALL on the Coombe was built in 1745–7 although projected as early as 1738. At that time the weaving industry of the Liberties was in decline. It replaced a hall of 1682. The upper storey, rebuilt in the nineteenth century, may have been designed with a pediment. The hall proper was wainscotted and measured 50 ft x 21 ft, containing a pair of fine carved chimneypieces and a tapestry in a carved frame depicting George II inscribed 'The Workmanship of John Vanbeaver Ye Famous Tapistry Weaver' and dated 1758. Vanbeaver also wove the House of Lords tapestries.

The weavers, anxious to draw themselves to the monarch's attention, commissioned a gilded lead statue from Benjamin Rackstrow (d. 1772), a hack London sculptor. It was unveiled in July 1750. The statue survived, albeit with a shaky left leg, until 1937 when it was destroyed during removal by a tenant. The head and boots are now in the Dublin Civic Museum. The tapestry was for many years in the possession of Messrs Atkinson and Co. (q.v.), the Dublin poplin manufacturers. It is now at the Metropolitan Museum of Art in New York.

The hall which in later years successively housed scrap metal, furniture and surplus clothing traders was demolished in 1956. The four storey weavers' almshouses which flanked it have also disappeared.

New Row Corner looking down Ward's Hill.

The gabled houses of the LIBERTIES reputedly survived longer than those elsewhere in the city because of the decline in the weaving industry in the eighteenth century and consequent lack of incentive to redevelop the area. Late nineteenth-century photographs show many of the houses in Weaver Square (none of which survive) already in a state of collapse.

Nearby Chamber Street seems to have been in better condition although the last of these houses has also gone, demolished in the 1950s. The houses, with triangular gables, dated from the turn of the eighteenth century and may be seen as a development of the earlier timber-framed gabled houses translated into brick.

The curvilinear gable or Dutch billy was a feature of later houses. Three fine examples dating from 1721 stood in Sweeney's Lane until 1932. Others stood in the vicinity of New Row and Newmarket. Curvilinear gables, often described as imported by the Low Country weavers, were, according to the author of a study of these houses, Mr Peter Walsh, in fact quite common in south-west England. The complexity of the gabled roofs left plenty of places for water penetration if badly maintained, as photographs of the buildings in decline show.

Note in the two views (*c.* 1900) of New Row how the gables on the corner house had been truncated. The photograph of Marrowbone Lane shows gabled houses opposite the old William Jameson distillery which has also disappeared.

Ward's Hill — New Row Corner, showing gables.

Sweeny's Lane.

102

Chamber Street.

Marrowbone Lane with William Jameson's distillery.

Weavers' Square.

Among the more imposing houses in the Liberties was the residence built by the Ward family about 1700 on what became known as WARD'S HILL. According to the Georgian Society Records, a Richard Ward, brewer, was living in New Row in 1680. The new house probably faced the brewery. At the time the photograph was taken, about 1900, the house was in tenements. It was owned by the Gibton family for many years. Some of the oak panelling in the hall survived until demolition. The remains of an orchard to the rear also survived into this century.

Peter Walsh has noted the similarities between this house and a gabled mansion in Marrowbone Lane (reputedly built in 1703 and demolished in 1813) illustrated by Ben Clayton in the *Dublin Penny Journal*. The curved coping line on the surviving flank wing was similar to that on the Clayton house, which echoed the curves of the Dutch-billy gable that rose a further two storeys. Whether or not the Ward house had such a gable must remain conjectural.

Wood Quay, now associated with more ancient settlements, was for generations of Dubliners best known for the remarkable stucco work on O'Meara's (formerly Timoney's) IRISH HOUSE at the corner of Winetavern Street. Built for Mr P. P. Kelly in 1870, the façade was decorated with Celtic revival and nationalist subjects by stuccodores Burnet and Comerford. Wolfhounds, 'methers' (ancient drinking cups) and the Stone of Destiny were set into niches in the pilasters surmounted by round towers. The cast ironwork of the balustrade incorporated the date and the mottoes 'Cead Mile Failte' and 'Erin Go Bragh'. In the first-floor panels on the Wood Quay façade were 'Rich and Rare', a maiden standing by a seated harpist, and Henry Grattan's 'Last Address to the Irish Parliament', while around the corner beyond the Kelly arms over the door were 'Erin Weeping on a Stringless Harp' and Daniel O'Connell.

The Irish House was demolished in the mid 1960s. The plaster figures were removed to the Guinness Museum.

The celebrated row of houses on MICHAEL'S HILL, Winetavern Street, each with a single large tripartite window at first and second-floor levels, dated from *c.* 1800. The entire block which extended further down the hill to Cook Street and backed onto Michael's Lane was occupied by generations of 'clothes brokers'. Originally called Christchurch Lane, to which there was a reference in 1354, the name change in the early nineteenth century came from its proximity to the Church of St Michael, the tower of which survives in the Synod Hall. Michael's Hill was demolished in 1964.

Michael's Hill.

Michael's Lane.

CHRIST CHURCH CATHEDRAL was photographed by Messrs Millard and Robinson in 1871 when G. E. Street's restoration was about to commence. The work was financed by Henry Roe, the distiller, and the Cathedral reopened for public service seven years later.

The view illustrated here was taken in Winetavern Street and shows the poor condition of the fabric at that time. The north wall of the nave, dating from the first quarter of the thirteenth century, had survived the collapse of the roof in 1652 which had taken the south arcade and aisle and much of the west end with it. Reconstruction failed to secure the northern half of the structure in any permanent way so that by 1766 a huge buttress had been built to support the west end. By 1871 the westernmost bay of clerestory windows had been blocked up to provide further stiffening.

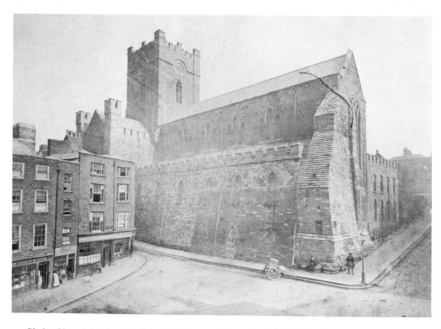

Christ Church Cathedral, from Winetavern Street in 1871 before G. E. Street's restoration.

Most incongruous was the massive battered wall erected along the north side with blind windows. When Street removed this he found early buttresses similar to those at Glastonbury Abbey, and he incorporated their detail in the new work. The addition of flying buttresses stabilised the fabric.

Street also rebuilt the west end, raised the tower (removing the clock erected in 1845 in place of an earlier one), remodelled the north transept and added crenellations to the nave — among other alterations. His most controversial demolition was the complete removal of the 100 ft long Long Choir in an effort to return the east end to its original layout.

A photograph of the interior of the choir looking towards the nave, from which it was separated by the organ loft and screen, is reproduced here. It was argued that while the choir dated from 1359, little original work survived. The four arches seen here were apparently twelfth century but much of the remainder dates from Matthew Price's cathedral restoration of 1831–3. In the exterior view can be seen the houses at the top of Winetavern Street, the first two of which had tripartite windows like those on the houses across the street (Michael's Hill q.v.). Like the Cathedral, these windows were badly affected by settlement. settlement.

Dublin's narrowest shop, in Winetavern Street, demolished 1949.

The corner house, J. Lawler, was subsequently taken down and its neighbour refronted with conventional paired windows. The next house (between Kelly and Taylor and J. Dundon) was Dublin's narrowest shop, only 7 feet from edge to edge. It was demolished in 1949. All the surrounding houses on this side of the street were cleared for the Civic Offices in the 1960s.

Christ Church Cathedral: the Long Choir before its removal by Street.

THE CHURCH OF ST JOHN THE EVANGELIST, Fishamble Street, was built in 1766–9 to the designs of George Ensor and stood a few yards north east of the old Long Choir of Christ Church Cathedral. The Parish of St John is mentioned as early as 1178. The church was enlarged in 1350 and rebuilt in the seventeenth and again in the seventeenth centuries. A spire added in 1639 was not retained in Ensor's design. His façade consisted of a pediment supported on four ionic columns in antis.

In 1877 the parish was united to St Werburgh's. While St John's closed in the following year it remained standing until 1884 when it was demolished as part of the Corporation's plan to link Dame Street with Christchurch Place.

MOLYNEUX HOUSE, Peter Street, was built in 1711 by Thomas Molyneux, physician-general to the army in Ireland and younger brother of the author of *The Case of Ireland Stated*. Its destruction in 1943 was described by Maurice Craig 'as one of the really regrettable losses Dublin as suffered in recent years'. The Molyneuxs had owned a house on New Row South, off Thomas Street, where Thomas was born in 1661.

The Peter Street house, which had a modillion cornice and centre pediment, marked a stylistic departure from the gabled type hitherto in vogue in the city. When Sir Thomas Molyneux, who was given a baronetcy in 1730, died in 1733, he left the house to his widow. It later passed to his second son who moved to Merrion Square in 1778. The Peter Street house was taken for a while by one William Lane and then in 1778 by Philip Astley the equestrian.

Astley had toured England performing 'feats and entertainments of horsemanship' with much success. He built an amphitheatre behind Molyneux House with an entrance to the pit and gallery in Bride Street. More affluent patrons entered their boxes by way of the house, which also served as Astley's residence. Astley's Amphitheatre soon became the most fashionable place of entertainment in Dublin, running 'musical pieces, dancing, tumbling and pantomime' in addition to equestrian spectaculars. In 1805, with business badly affected by the post-Union decline, Astley let it for a season to Charles and Thomas Dibdin.

Astley left for London in 1809 selling out for £6,000 to a Scot, Henry Erskine Johnstone, who opened it as the 'Royal Hibernian Theatre' in November of that year. Johnstone got into debt and absconded in 1812. For almost fifty years from 1815 Molyneux House served as an asylum for blind women. Between 1862 and 1907, when it was known as Albert House, the inmates were aged

Molyneux House, Peter Street.

women. Its last occupants were the Salvation Army. Among the features which survived into their tenure was the panelled hall, seen here, and the richly-carved staircase. The adjoining amphitheatre which had been converted into a chapel for the inmates was altered and partly rebuilt following the removal of the blind institution to Leeson Street in 1862. The perpendicular gothic façade which survived until comparatively recently was probably added before this date however.

In 1941, having lain disused for some six years, the chapel was sold and adapted as Messrs Jacob's Recreation Hall. In 1974 it was acquired by Stephenson Gibney and Associates and converted to house their architectural practice.

Molyneux House, hall detail.

CANON STREET, off Bride Street, was reputedly Dublin's shortest street, having just one address — the public house of Messrs Rutledge and Sons. It was also the venue for the Bird Market. The name came from the minor canons of St Patrick's Cathedral, hence its early (1754) name of Petty Canon Alley. Rutledge's was pulled down in the early 1960s when Bride Street was widened.

NOS. 4 AND 5 GREAT LONGFORD STREET were the last pair of curvilinear gabled houses in Dublin to survive with their gables unaltered. They were probably contemporary with the Sweeney's Lane houses (1721), having flat-headed doorways and a similar plan with narrow hallways, L-shaped back rooms and central stacks. The stack, a massive affair (with perhaps eighteen flues) had been truncated many years ago.

Dr Craig illustrated the houses with a sketch plan and elevations in his *Dublin 1660–1860* and drew attention to their importance. A statement published in the newspapers in 1951 that they were to be preserved as the last of their type proved regrettably to be unfounded.

NOS. 7 AND 8 GREAT SHIP STREET, illustrated in the Georgian Society Records by both photograph and drawing (by Sir T. M. Deane) were among the most interesting house pairs in the city. The doorways with Gibbs surround were capped by a single pediment on brackets, and flanked on each elevation by Venetian windows lighting the ground-floor rooms. They stood on the west side of the street opposite Dublin Castle; they disappeared in the late 1950s.

Perhaps no Dublin façade has suffered more than that of ST WERBURGH'S CHURCH which dates back to the rebuilding of 1715—19 and of which only the lower stage survives today. No architect's name is known although it bears a remarkable resemblance to the façade of St Ann's, Dawson Street (q.v.), as projected by Isaac Wills in 1720 but never completed.

Both façades owe much to Roman churches. Although Thomas Burgh was concerned in its construction, Dr Rolf Loeber thinks that the design (derived from da Volterra's Santa Chiara, Rome) may pre-date his first involvement in 1713. In 1729 an octagonal tower was added above the west end, and two years later capped by a wooden dome and cross paid for by Doctors Synge and Delany. In 1754 the roof, dome and church interior were gutted by fire. It was rebuilt and re-opened in 1759. In 1768 a tower and spire of 160 feet were added to a totally new design incorporating Wren elements.

In 1810 the spire was taken down allegedly because it was unstable. However, a glance at Malton's engraving of the upper Castle Yard illustrates the fears felt by the authorities in the aftermath of the Emmet rising about any potential sniping point in the vicinity. The tower proper and the upper section of the façade were taken down in 1836. The bells were later dispersed to other churches.

STATE APARTMENTS, DUBLIN CASTLE: In January 1941 fire swept through the suite of drawing-rooms in the south-east range of the Upper Castle Yard. The roof collapsed, destroying the ceilings of two rooms: one coved, the other flat and compartmented and thought to have been designed by Sir Edward Lovett Pearce in 1732. (He had been responsible for the temporary ballroom decoration at the Castle in the previous year.) This range effectively consisted of two buildings built back to back. That fronting onto the yard was built early in the eighteenth century as a continuation of the south-west range designed by Sir William Robinson in 1685.

Pearce is believed to have built the stone-faced extension looking out on the Castle gardens and linked to the older work by a central corridor, originally top lit, which resembles his work at the Parliament House. This corridor was also damaged by the fire. Restoration work on the Upper Castle Yard began with the re-building in 1961–4 from the ground up of the cross block which abutted the burnt-out range and had been taken down in 1958 because of sinking foundations. The cross block, originally built about 1716, had persistently suffered from settlement. In 1796 Austin Cooper, the antiquarian, observed the demolition of the northern half of the block which had cracked some years earlier owing, he thought, to inadequate filling in the Castle Ditch.

It was decided not to replace the fine drawing-room with the coved ceiling which had occupied the four end bays next to the Throne Room. The second drawing-room with the flat ceiling was reproduced in facsimile and fitted out with the pier glasses and console tables salvaged from the fire. (Two fireplaces in the room had come from a house in Ely Place in the 1890s.) The range was rebuilt to the west of its original location, with two screened ante-rooms instead of the original one, so that the space occupied by the drawing-rooms (a total of eleven bays) was now occupied by one of ten bays. On the original plan there was a back stairs in the twelfth bay.

The two-bay room which now remained in the angle next to the cross block was found to be of the same dimensions as that of an early eighteenth-century panelled interior, the Apollo Room salvaged from Tracton House (q.v.) in St Stephen's Green in 1912 and displayed until 1944 in the National Museum. The ceiling and other fittings from Tracton House were successfully reinstated while the panelling was copied from the original.

The restoration of the State Apartments, which included the refacing of the façade attributed to Pearce and the installation of plasterwork salvaged from Mespil House in the late 1940s, earned a Silver Medal from the Royal Institute of the Architects of Ireland for the architects in charge, Oscar Richardson, J. B. Maguire and the late Raymond McGrath.

110

LA TOUCHE BANK, Castle Street, was built before 1735 and possibly begun eight years earlier. In August 1726 David La Touche leased from the Corporation a 49 ft wide strip of land fronting onto the south side of Castle Street. This date would tie in with Dr Craig's attribution to Sir Edward Lovett Pearce, arguably Ireland's greatest Palladian architect.

The building, which probably served initially as both a bank and a private house, was five bays wide and rose three storeys over a rusticated granite ground floor and two levels of basements. Wings were added in 1802–3, to the designs of Sir Richard Morrison. In 1870 the La Touche family, who had been in business in Dublin since 1701, sold out to the Munster Bank who occupied the premises during the construction of their new offices on Dame Street. Empty from 1874–8, it was purchased by the government and used by the Veterinary Department of the Privy Council.

Most of the building was taken down in the autumn of 1945. The lower part of the front wall was left standing and may still be seen. The Venus ceiling from the back boudoir was re-erected in the directors' luncheon room of the Bank of Ireland, commemorating the strong links between the La Touche family and the Bank; Rt Hon. David La Touche was its first governor.

PIM BROTHERS & CO WAREHOUSE SOUTH Gt GEORGES St DUBLIN.

MESSRS PIM'S department store in South Great George's Street, acquired about 1843 and rebuilt in several phases from the 1850s onwards to the designs of Sandham Symes (1806—94), was that family's first business venture away from South William Street where they had operated a number of companies.

Later in the century they were the chief instigators of the South City Markets project and the development of most of South Great George's Street from Stephen's Street to the Central Hotel, including much of Exchequer Street. The store and adjoining block were demolished in the 1970s for office development.

112

The illustrations show the SOUTH CITY MARKETS, South Great George's Street, in their original form. After just eleven years of existence, they were severely damaged by fire in 1892 and rebuilt without the market hall and pyramid towers. The project was conceived by a group of Dublin businessmen in 1875. In the following year a bill was passed at Westminster enabling them to acquire the properties in the block bounded by South Great George's Street, Exchequer Street, Drury Street and Fade Street. The centre of the site had been the site of the original Castle Market of 1704, reopened in 1783 as the New Castle Market with butchers' stalls and slaughterhouses along an avenue extending into South William Street. By the 1870s the area had greatly declined and was reputedly one of the most unhealthy parts of the city.

In 1878 ten firms were invited to submit designs under motto in an architectural competition to be judged by Alfred Waterhouse ARA, a noted London architect. The winning scheme, entitled 'Northern Light', was entered by Messrs Lockwood and Mawson of Bradford. The elevations bore an uncanny resemblance to 'Labor Omnia Vincit' with which they had won the Nottingham University Buildings competition two years earlier, when the adjudicator had been the same Mr Waterhouse. In fact the style of the South City Markets was close to some of Waterhouse's own creations.

The principal feature of the building was the vast iron and glass central market hall based on Lockwood and Mawson's Kirkgate Market (built 1871—7) in Bradford. The venture was not a success. The opening in 1881 was interrupted by crowds protesting at the arrest of Parnell some days earlier. In the following year the *Irish Builder*, which had been biased from the moment English architects had been selected (compounded by the appointment of English contractors and subcontractors), predicted the failure of the venture due to a public boycott.

In order to save it, half of the hall was partitioned off as Messrs Pim's Furniture Emporium with an entrance from Exchequer Street. The Pim family had been the principal promotors of the scheme. Early on the morning of 27 August 1892 the greater portion of the markets was destroyed by a fire which started in the hall and spread rapidly among the stalls. One newspaper reported that 'it seemed as if an enormous tar barrel had been set alight in the centre of the city'. Although the market hall collapsed together with portions of the Drury Street and Exchequer Street frontages, the fire was prevented from spreading to the bonded store underneath.

The South City Markets were rebuilt under the supervision of William H. Byrne, but with two intersecting arcades instead of a central hall. The surviving pyramid towers over the Fade Street and George's Street entrances were taken down. The Royal Arcade on Manningham Lane, Bradford, was built in 1897 with a virtually identical façade, albeit in stone, to the Dublin design submitted almost twenty years earlier. It was presumably the work of the same firm, by then known as Mawson and Hudson.

This photograph of EXCHEQUER STREET was taken about 1879 for the promoters of the South City Markets, built facing the buildings seen here. They later acquired and rebuilt much of this side too. The old Exchequer was situated on or near this street. In 1728 it appears as Chequer Lane. The premises of J. Hendrick, provision dealer at No. 39 (note the bottles in the yard) has the appearance of a shanty, not unusual in Dublin even at this late date (for example, No. 80 Dorset Street q.v.) Mansfield, on the site now occupied by Central Hotel Chambers, was a grocer and Patrick Lynch, at No. 37, a furniture broker. The pedimented gateway further down was the entrance to the premises of Messrs Drake and McComas, rectifying distillers, wine, tea and general import merchants.

CUFFE STREET was named for Sir James Cuffe MP who married Alice Aungier in 1655. While the street is shown on a 1685 map, it was probably not built upon until after this date. Most of the eighteenth-century houses, including some early gabled examples, have now been demolished, much of the north side for flats. The Stephen's Green end disappeared in the 1970s for road widening. The tall building with a cupola on the skyline in the photograph was the old Kevin Street Technical School, by W. M. Mitchell, built in 1887 and replaced by the new college in the 1960s. Mitchell's Kevin Street Library, later but in a similar style, survives.

Today little is left of Georgian YORK STREET, once a fashionable address but whose decline, despite proximity to St Stephen's Green, paralleled that of the Gardiner Estate north of the Liffey. Among the nineteenth-century residents were the architects W. V. Morrison and E. H. Carson. It appears on Brooking's Map of 1728. Roque's Map, published twenty-eight years later, shows it mostly built up.

On the south side at the corner of Little Cuffe Street (now Mercer Street) there was a tennis-court in the seventeenth century which stood behind the mansion of the Earls of Abercorn on St Stephen's Green (q.v.). The widow of the 6th Earl let 'a piece of ground called the Old Tennis Court' in 1740 which by 1756 had been built upon. The garden immediately behind the house was sold in 1808 to Rev. Albert Nesbitt DD, who built an independent chapel (later York Street Congregational Church) on the site. The shell of this building survives as the Salvation Army Hostel. The houses between it and Mercer Street were reconstructed by the Corporation in the late 1940s. The north side opposite is now entirely occupied by the Royal College of Surgeons who first came here in 1805 when they acquired the old Quaker burial ground at the corner of the Green and expanded northwards and westwards later in the century.

The photograph, taken in 1948, shows Nos. 33—45 where the modern extension to the College now stands. The houses at the far side of the Mercer Street junction, illustrated by Flora Mitchell in *Vanishing Dublin*, were demolished in 1964—6. The doric pedimented doorcase appears to have been a York Street feature. Many survive on the Corporation houses.

IX

SOUTH EAST CITY, BALLSBRIDGE AND RINGSEND

HARCOURT STREET was laid out about 1775 by John Hatch, Seneschal of the Manor of St Sepulchre and was named for the then Lord Lieutenant, the 1st Earl Harcourt. Much of the fabric of the street was replaced in the 1970s by office blocks with facsimile façades. Many of these houses had ended their days as family-run hotels.

Among the larger houses was No. 40, John Hatch's own residence, seen here at the left during demolition in 1977. Hatch died here in October 1797. It was later the home of his son-in-law Rev. Sir Samuel Synge Hutchinson, who died in 1846. The next resident was Rt Hon. Rev. Henry Packenham, Dean of St Patrick's. It was then the home for more than a century of The High School (now removed to Rathgar), one of several grammar schools supported by the Erasmus Smith endowments. No. 40 was a double-fronted house with, unusually for Dublin, round-headed windows at ground-floor level. A new block, scheduled to be built on the site, will have a replica façade.

ALEXANDRA COLLEGE was opened at No. 6 Earlsfort Terrace in October 1866 as Queen's College. In 1874 No. 5, which had been the home of Mrs Jellicoe, the headmistress, and No. 7, the residence of Judge Thomas Lefroy, were acquired. A new hall and theatre — 'Jellicoe Hall' — was opened in 1879 and it was greatly enlarged with the addition of two extra storeys and other alterations in 1900.

In the intervening years a further three houses in Earlsfort Terrace and two in Lower Leeson Street were taken in. In 1889 Alexandra School, which had been founded at 72–73 St Stephen's Green some sixteen years earlier, moved to a new building by W. Kaye Parry (1853–1932) which had been erected next door to the College. As completed, the two buildings complemented each other with ornate brick façades and slate roofs topped by flèches.

In 1972, following the relocation of the school and college in new buildings at Dartry, the entire Earlsfort Terrace site, which had grown to take in a further terrace to the north, was cleared. The Clergy Daughters School at No. 12, designed by Lanyon, Lynn & Lanyon in 1863 and formerly the residence of Archbishop Plunket, was also levelled. Plans to build an office block development, since revised to include an hotel, have yet to be realised.

Alexandra College before 1900. Note the Royal University campanile, later moved to Kildare Place (q.v.).

Alexandra College showing the additions carried out in 1900.

116

The foundation stone of ST
MATTHIAS'S CHURCH, Upper
Hatch Street, was laid by Archbishop Whately on St Matthias's
Day, 24 February 1842. The site,
part of the proposed Wellington
Square, was given rent free together
with a sum of £500 by Rev. Sir
Samuel Synge Hutchinson. The
architect was Daniel Robertson
who came to Ireland in 1829
following an unspecified scandal
at Oxford where he had designed
the University Press and other
buildings. Although he had a very
successful country-house practice
working, as he did, in both the
classical and Tudor Gothic styles,
this was his only known Irish
church.

The main north façade, a tetra-
style Greek corinthian portico,
faced down a lawn to Hatch Street
while the plain rear faced Adelaide
Road. In December 1843, shortly
after the opening of the church for
worship, Robertson made designs
for adding a clerk's living accommodation and belfry to the south
front. It is not clear how much of
this scheme was carried out. A
barrel-vaulted chancel and transepts
were added in 1851. The gallery, lit
by ox-eye windows, had box pews
and was supported on cast-iron
columns.

The Wellington Square project
came to nothing. Part of the square
proper was taken into the church
grounds while the adjoining lands
to the west were sold to the Dublin
Wicklow and Wexford Railway in
the 1850s. Only two houses (demolished in 1980) were built on
the railway land on Upper Hatch
Street; the remainder was occupied
by Harcourt Street Station. St
Matthias's was demolished in the
late 1950s.

EARLSFORT TERRACE was broken through into St Stephen's Green with the demolition in 1839 of a row of small gabled houses at the bottom of Lesson Street, Yet by as late as 1878 only two houses (centre right, dating from the 1840s) had been built on the upper section between Hatch Street and Adelaide Road. By the close of the century, however, both sides were complete.

In the late 1970s most of the east side was redeveloped, including the Diocesan School for Girls on the corner (right foreground) and 21—22 Earlsfort Mansions, reputedly the first commercial apartment block in the city and erected by Alderman Pile in the 1880s. Only two houses, Nos. 17 and 18, survive on this side. Opposite, the Earlsfort Hotel as well as Nos. 25 and 26 also went in the 1970s as did Crawford's Garage (formerly Brittain's) which was originally built as a skating rink and which is fronted in this view by what looks like a row of cottages.

PLEASANTS' ASYLUM, 75 Lower Camden Street, was opened in 1818 for the daughters of reduced citizens of the united parishes of St Peter and St Kevin, and within three years had twenty-one inmates. It was built and funded with monies left by Thomas Pleasants, a Carlow-born philanthropist who disbursed some £100,000 to charity. He erected the Stove Tenter House for the Dublin weavers in 1815 and paid for the operating room at the Meath Hospital and for the lodges at the Botanic Gardens, in addition to making donations to the Royal Dublin Society.

In 1949 Pleasants' Asylum amalgamated with Kirwan House (q.v.) on the North Circular Road. The plaque over the front door of the Asylum, recording the names of the three first governors appointed by the Court—Rev. Thomas Gamble, Joshua Pasley and Samuel Coates, was moved to the grounds of Kirwan House. Upper floors of the former Asylum may still be seen above modern shop fronts.

While Dublin Georgian houses sometimes presented a fairly bland uniform façade to the street, particularly when the Wide Street Commissioners were at work, their rear elevations often displayed remarkable variety of composition. Witness these examples in CHARLEMONT STREET, demolished between the wars and photographed by the Georgian Society about 1910.

118

This turf boat is being unloaded on the Grand Canal at GRAND PARADE. In the nineteenth century turf was carried to the city from the midlands in quantities of up to 40,000 tons per annum. During the Emergency some 200,000 tons of turf and briquettes were carried to Dublin by canal.

In the background is the metal bridge erected by the Dublin and Wicklow Railway Company over which the first train to Bray ran, from a temporary terminus at Harcourt Street, on 10 July 1854. George Wilkinson's Harcourt Street Station, the terminus for the line, was not opened until February 1859. Following the closure of the line almost exactly a hundred years later, this and the other bridges were removed; parts of the embankment remain.

To the left can be seen part of Charlemont Place dating from about 1806 and demolished from the mid 1960s onwards. The second view shows Charlemont Place after the removal of the bridge. Several other streets in the neighbourhood disappeared in recent years, among them Peter Place (pre-1821), entered through gates on Adelaide Road. The nearby house (Janeville) and extensive gardens of the Peter family have also gone.

119

THE MAGDALEN ASYLUM, Lower Leeson Street, which opened on 11 June 1766 was founded by the 'pious and amiable Lady Arabella Denny, for unfortunate females abandoned by their seducers, and rejected by their friends, who preferred a life of penitence and virtue to one of guilt, infamy and prostitution'. Many of the inmates had been brought up in the Foundling Hospital Charter Schools. Lady Arabella, the daughter of the 1st Earl of Kerry, was widowed in 1740. A friend and neighbour of Mrs Delany of Delville (q.v.), in 1759 she enlisted the aid of her social acquaintances in helping 'destitute children' in the Foundling Hospital. Before long she found herself working alone but succeeded in improving conditions. She continued to work at the hospital while running the asylum.

The asylum chapel, the principal generator of revenue, was opened for service in 1768 when an 'excellent sermon' preached by Dean Bayley raised £150 from the fashionable congregation. Initially admission was by ticket only, children being discouraged from attending the charity sermons 'to reserve as much room as possible for the benefactors'. The chapel was galleried with box pews and an apsidal east (or rather west) end. It was extended twice, raising the accommodation from five to seven hundred. An account of 1821 noted that 'the institution is much indebted to the Latouche family'.

In 1868, presumably to keep pace with ecclesiological fashions, a new front in the romanesque style was added from the designs of J. Rawson Carroll (1830–1911). The principal feature, the tower which had a slate spire decorated with cast-iron crockets, became a landmark in the locale, visible from St Stephen's Green and at the end of the long vista from the canal. The Magdalen Asylum was acquired in the late 1950s by Comhlucht Siúicre Éireann who erected an office block on the site to Boyle and Delaney's competition-winning design.

120

BAGGOT STREET LOWER saw some notable changes during the 1970s, including the building of the Bank of Ireland headquarters on the site formerly occupied in part by motor assemblers, Lincoln and Nolan, which in the nineteenth century had housed Thomas Denehy's coach building works. The houses of Adelaide Place, acquired by Lincoln and Nolan in the late 1950s and early sixties, have also gone. They can be seen on the left in the Lawrence view of the 'College' shown here — part of the Mercy Convent — which has been replaced by a modern school building.

Baggot Street, so called as early as 1773, included later buildings in the Georgian style. The terrace to the right of the temple bore a plaque with the legend 'New Buildings A.D. 1862 — G.A.'. The plaque was re-erected in 1978 when a facsimile office block was built on the site. The temple to the left was the First Church of Christ Scientist, built in 1934 and demolished forty years later. Its railings survive in front of the Bord na Mona headquarters. The houses to the left of it were demolished in the early 1960s for one of Dublin's first modern office blocks, the Bord Fáilte building.

Lincoln & Nolan's.

Adelaide Place.

In 1893 the ROYAL CITY OF DUBLIN HOSPITAL in Baggot Street was rebuilt and enlarged by the architect Albert E. Murray (1849–1924). The new façade was described by the *Irish Builder* as 'late and flat – with a strong turn in the gables towards the Dutch', and was faced, like many other Murray buildings, with red Ruabon brick and buff terracotta – known to Dublin wags as 'Murray's Mellow Mixture'.

The building it replaced, shown here, reputedly began life as a row of houses purchased in 1831 by a group of professors from the College of Surgeons, 'for the purpose of affording additional hospital relief to the sick and poor of the metropolis'. The purchase was the culmination of several attempts to found a teaching hospital attached to the College. A special wing for the treatment of fevers and contagious diseases was added in 1868, from the designs of Charles Geoghegan, with funds left by Alderman John Drummond.

While MOUNT STREET LOWER dates from 1790, the group shown here at the corner of Warrington Place was somewhat later, being built in 1814. In fact, building carried on here into the 1820s. The origin of the name, Haliday suggested, was the 'rocky gallows mount' near Baggot Street Lower. It may not be coincidence, however, that there was already in existence a fashionable street in London of the same name.

Much of Mount Street, in parts decayed, disappeared in the late 1960s and 1970s for office development. Most of the surviving houses are located at the western end next to Merrion Square.

LEA HOUSE, No. 93 Pembroke Road, was in many respects typical of the large red-brick semi-detached houses built in Ballsbridge in the 1860s and 1870s. It was unusual in that one-half of it was in a different street, No. 42 Elgin Road. They were built about 1872 on a large site at the angle between the two roads. Lea House served for many years as the offices of the Irish Tourist Board. The pair were acquired in 1956 by the Embassy of the United States and were removed to make way for the new chancellery.

For over seventy years HAMMERSMITH WORKS on Pembroke Road, Ballsbridge was the headquarters of the building firm of G. & T. Crampton who moved there from Great Brunswick Street in 1892 and built Hume House on its site in the 1960s. The name Hammersmith dates back long before Crampton's time, to 1834, when Richard Turner (1798–1881), ironmonger, of 4 St Stephen's Green took a lease on a 200 ft by 200 ft site in Pembroke Road to the east of the Trinity College Botanic Gardens, from the Honourable Sidney Herbert. Turner moved into a dwelling house which he named Hammersmith on the west end of the site. With other buildings, it had recently been erected there for £1,400 by a doctor named George Davy who seems to have got into financial difficulties.

In 1835 Turner began to describe himself as a manufacturer rather than ironmonger. Four years later he cast the iron frames for the Palm House at the Belfast Botanic Gardens and supervised its construction. In the 1840s he built a series of conservatories — at the Vice-Regal Lodge 1840 (demolished), Glasnevin Botanic Gardens (extensions 1845 onwards) and the Winter Garden in Regent's Park. In this last, and in his masterpiece, the Palm House at Kew (1844–8), he worked with the architect Decimus Burton. He shared competition honours with an entry for the Great Exhibition Building, London, in 1850, and was furious when a design subsequently submitted by Paxton secured the contract. Paxton even copied Turner's transepts in execution.

Among the railway sheds Turner designed and constructed were Westland Row and the Broadstone (1847) in Dublin, and Lime Street (1847–50) in Liverpool. He also built several important conservatories for private clients in Ireland and Scotland, including Killakee, Co. Dublin (demolished) and probably also Ballyfin, Co. Laois, currently under threat. Although he remained involved, from 1857 Hammersmith Works was run by his son William.

In 1876 the lease was sold to the Hammersmith Skating Rink Company, which folded after a year. Although the ironworks was moved to North King Street, William Turner continued to reside at Hammersmith House until his death in 1888. The house with its cast-iron verandahs and conservatories was something of an advertisement for the firm. The royal arms over the Works entrance were of cast iron, as was no doubt the belfry seen through the archway.

Hammersmith House, subsequently renamed Melrose, served for many years as the residence of the principal of the Veterinary College, built behind it at the turn of the century. Abandoned in the 1930s, it was demolished in about 1956 for an extension to the College. Turner's Cottages, built at the rear of the Works, survived up to the early 1970s.

MARINE SCHOOL.

Published according to Act of Parliament March 1 1779.

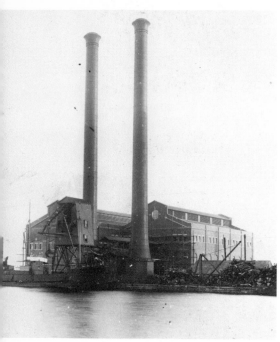

In 1770 the Governors of the Hibernian Nursery for the Support and Education of the Orphans and Children of Mariners took out a lease on a plot of land on Sir John Rogerson's Quay with the intention of building a new school to replace the house in Ringsend which they had out-grown after just four years of occupation. The cost of erection, £6,600, was defrayed by Parliament. The new HIBERNIAN MARINE SCHOOL opened in 1773. A charter was obtained two years later.

Although Malton gives the architect as Thomas Ivory, other authorities attribute it to Thomas Cooley. The building was faced with granite ashlar with a rusticated ground floor. The chapel and the school-room, each 51 ft by 26 ft, were located in the left and right wings respectively. Although the charter claimed accommodation for two hundred boys, only a hundred and sixty could be housed — and the actual numbers in the house were in practice somewhat lower than this. An inquiry into conditions in the 1820s led to the termination of Parliamentary grants and a reduction in numbers.

In 1872 the interior of the main block was burnt out. The school moved to new premises. Three years later Sir Richard Martin, the timber merchant, moved in to Rogerson's Quay. His firm used only the out-offices although the main house seems to have been patched up. The firm amalgamated with T. & C. Martin and left the premises in the 1920s. In 1934 the chapel was observed to be intact but unsafe. After a period of occupation by the B+I Line the premises were converted to a cold store. In 1979, after several years of disuse, the main building was demolished. The wings survive in a stripped state. One was reroofed in 1980.

The cruciform-plan LOCK KEEPER'S HOUSE on the spit of land between the Grand Canal Docks and the mouth of the Dodder was erected by the Canal company in 1805. It was replaced by a modern house in 1944. The keeper had charge of three locks, Camden, Buckingham and Westmoreland, which opened in 1795 and which survive in varying states of repair. Camden, the widest, is that seen in the photograph. Although the docks were built to accommodate 150 sea-going vessels, they were not successful commercially. The proximity of the Dodder causes silting, while the advent of the paddle-steamer, which was too wide for the locks, greatly limited their attraction.

THE TRAMWAY TWINS: In 1900 an American construction company began work on a new power station for the lately reconstituted Dublin United Tramways Co. Ltd on the south bank of the Grand Canal Docks next to the Ringsend Road. The first electric tram ran on the Dublin Southern Districts Tramways Co. line between Haddington Road and Dalkey in 1896. The D.U.T.C. opposed their rival's plans to extend their electric line and enlisted the support of the city's jarveys. Eventually they bought out the D.S.D.T.C. and set up a new company under the chairmanship of William Martin Murphy. The former D.S.D.T.C. power station at Shelbourne Road was soon joined by the second on the system — at Clontarf, opened in 1897.

Both of these were closed when the Ringsend station, capable of powering the whole system, opened in 1906. The complex, consisting of adjoining boiler-house and engine room, was dominated by two concrete-lined steel stacks visible from many parts of the city and dubbed 'The Tramway Twins'.

With the advent of the Shannon scheme the coal-burning station was rendered uneconomic. It was taken over by the E.S.B. and maintained intact but disused until September 1932 when it was decided to remove the plant. In the autumn of the following year a tender was received for £50 from one Jack George for the removal of the chimneys: the scrap value must have been considered high. Nothing was done however. At about the same time the contents of the boiler-house were removed to garage buses, a decision to clear out the engine room being deferred.

In 1934 the firm of William Hunter and Sons began the painstaking task of dismantling the stacks with pneumatic drills and oxyacetylene equipment, reckoned to be a twelve-month job. They were considered too resilient to pull with hawsers and likely to rebound and explode when toppled. Hunters succeeded in removing half of the west chimney before giving up and it was not until 1943 that the attempt was renewed, the job being completed by Hammond Lane. The buildings were sold in January 1939 to Brittains, the car assemblers. They were vacated in the mid-1960s and were subsequently demolished.

X

SOUTH SUBURBS

Among the most interesting Dublin buildings erected in the international style in the 1930s was the IMCO cleaning and dyeing works on Merrion Road. The firm was founded in 1927 by the Spiro family and expanded rapidly. The original reinforced concrete structure was unremarkable but was extended with the addition of a steel-framed stair tower encased in concrete and glass to the designs of the English architect Oliver Percy Bernard (1881–1939) and completed after his death by his executant architects Messrs Higginbotham and Stafford. Bernard is best remembered for the remarkable art deco interior of the Strand Palace Hotel, London, removed in 1968.

In June 1939 Imco announced plans for the construction of extra accommodation including bomb-proof shelters. In the post-war era trends changed in the dry-cleaning business. By the 1960s the concept of a centralised plant had become an anachronism. Imco diversified into shops and in 1974 sold the Merrion Road premises for office development.

While the shell of FRESCATI, Blackrock, stands, the house was so extensively vandalised while empty during the 1970s that a photograph of it in pristine condition merits inclusion here. It was the favourite residence of Lord Edward Fitzgerald who in a letter of 1793 wrote: 'I am sitting in the bay window with all those pleasant feelings which the fine weather, the pretty place, the singing birds, the pretty wife and Frescati give me'. Five years later Lord Edward was captured and fatally wounded in Thomas Street.

The house was occupied by the Dowager Duchess of Leinster until 1802, then briefly owned by Sir Henry Cavendish, Receiver-General for Ireland. It served for a time as Mr Craig's Boys School, was greatly extended and then sold and subdivided into separate houses. Among the later residents were Field Marshal Sir Henry Wilson, Henry James Dudgeon, the stockbroker and, in more recent times, businessman Benjamin McKinley. In April 1981 the wings were demolished as part of a scheme to reconstruct the centre part of the shell.

MARETIMO, Blackrock, was built about 1778 by Sir Nicholas Lawless, MP for Lifford. A successful Dublin woollen merchant, he bought a peerage in 1789 and sat in the House of Lords as Baron Cloncurry of Cloncurry, Co. Kildare. Maretimo was, like its neighbouring marine villas — Blackrock House, home of Sir Harcourt Lees and Lord Clonmel's Neptune, well known for its round-the-clock entertainments and garden parties. On one memorable occasion when rain forced the guests indoors, Cloncurry had tables set up in the hall and bedrooms. His social whirl failed to advance him in the nobility, however. One commentator said of him: 'His person has more of the stiffness of a French dancing-master than of the easy disengaged air of a well-bred gentleman.' At the time of his death in 1799, his estates, including Lyons in Co. Kildare, were bringing in an annual income of £12,000.

His second son, Valentine, who succeeded him, was a member of the directory of the United Irishmen (though he later denied this) and an anti-union pamphleteer. It was he who persuaded the Dublin and Kingstown Railway Company, who wanted to transverse the lands of Maretimo, to build a bathing temple and an elaborate bridge, the 'Cloncurry towers', which still stands. Maretimo remained in the hands of the family until the death of the Hon. Frederick Lawless in the late 1920s. With the death of the 4th Baron some years later, the title died out. The house survived until the early 1970s, when it was replaced by a block of flats.

THE SALTHILL HOTEL, Monkstown, was built near the site of the ancient dún of Dun Laoghaire and began life as a private house. In 1834 the new railway between Dublin and Kingstown was opened with a station at Salthill. A contemporary journal stated: 'The house at Salthill is now converting, with vast additions, into a splendid tavern, which will rival its celebrated namesake in the vicinity of Eton College, in all, it is to be hoped, except its extravagant charges; and the hill itself will be cut into beautiful terraces and slants, and planted in an ornamental manner'. The architect was John Skipton Mulvany (1813–70).

The hotel stood virtually at the terminus of the railway line which initially went only as far as the west pier. Among its early visitors was William Thackeray who recorded his impressions in the *Irish Sketchbook*. In 1865 the operators, the Parry family, spent £5,000 on alterations and additions, including the picturesque tower, from the designs of John McCurdy. In 1907 the Salthill Hotel was advertised as 'convenient by Train and Electric Tram which pass Exhibition Grounds (i.e. Herbert Park). New Sanitary arrangements, and redecorated throughout'. It closed in the 1960s and was subsequently demolished to make way for flats.

THE KINGSTOWN MARINE GAR-
DENS PAVILION was built in
1903 from the designs of Kaye
Parry Ross and Owen, the firm
responsible for the Dublin Exhibition held in Herbert Park in the
same year. No doubt they were
extremely proficient in designing
timber buildings. Beneath the glass
and timber cladding, the Pavilion
had a steel and iron frame.

The design was suitably marine,
with tiers of promenade decks surmounted by Moghul corner turrets —
all painted with fire-proof paint.
The other precautions included
a fire main around the exterior
and strategically placed 'nests of
buckets'. The interior consisted
principally of a rectangular auditorium used at different times as
a skating rink and a concert hall
with seating for 1,000 patrons.
It was surrounded by internal
galleries on three sides and had
a 35 ft wide stage. Other rooms
included a tea-room, smoking-
room and ladies' and gentlemen's
reading-rooms.

The four-acre Marine Gardens,
complete with bandstand and water-
fall, were lit at night by coloured
lamps. The Pavilion was destroyed
by fire in November 1915. It was
rebuilt in the following year but
later replaced by a cinema, the
successsor to which (now the
Pavilion Theatre) still stands.

ST MICHAEL'S CHURCH, DUN LAOGHAIRE, dating from 1824, was a simple cruciform building with a belfry at the east end. In the 1870s J. J. McCarthy was brought in to rebuild the church in the grand manner that had earned him the title 'the Irish Pugin'. The old tower was retained, and stood until 1894 when J. L. Robinson (1847/8–94) built a more suitable tower and spire to the south of the original. However, it was not until the early years of the present century that the ensemble was completed when a row of shops that had obscured the west front was demolished, and an entrance made to Georges Street.

In July 1965 the body of the church was destroyed by fire, the timber roof being rapidly consumed, leaving only the spire untouched. The nave walls left standing were subsequently taken down and some of the cut stonework was used to face the new church built on the site. The tower and spire have been retained and are now free-standing.

GRANITE HALL, Glenageary Road, was built as a speculation in about 1821 by George Smith, contractor to the new asylum harbour at Dunleary/Kingstown. The house, which was faced completely with granite ashlar, cost £10,000. Smith owned a number of quarries in the area including one in the grounds of his own residence, Stone View (now Clarinda Park House). He owned seven houses on Glenageary Hill and the lands of Newtownsmith. Granite Hall, which stood in landscaped grounds overlooking Scotsman's Bay, was let to one Michael Keogh.

Following George Smith's death in 1825, the property passed to his son Samuel. In 1840 Keogh sold his leasehold interest for £3,000 to John Lewis O'Ferrall D.L., Commissioner of the Metropolitan Police, who moved here from Rockfield, Blackrock. His daughter, Ellen Letitia, married the Rt Hon. Charles Owen O'Conor, the O'Conor Donn, and took over the house in 1881. The O'Conor Donn died in 1906, and his widow in 1931. Granite Hall was sold to a builder, who occupied the house while developing the lands. It was subsequently the home of the McEnroe family and later the Minch family. It was demolished in the 1950s by another developer.

128

GLENAGEARY HOUSE began as a relatively modest residence, but it had already been enlarged with the addition of end wings before it was acquired by the stockbroker, Haliday Bruce, in 1842. Ten years later he made extensive improvements, adding an octagonal stair tower based on the Athenian Tower of the Winds. On the upper storey was an observation room with views over south County Dublin. Bruce probably added also the ionic colonnade at this time. Stylistically, there is reason to believe that he employed John Skipton Mulvany, architect of Dun Laoghaire railway station and the Royal Irish Yacht Club.

Following Bruce's death in 1857, the property was sold to Thomas Pim, one of the Pim Brothers of South Great Georges Street. In 1903 it was acquired by Alfred J. Waller, an undertaker and horse-driving enthusiast. Between the wars Glenageary House was converted into flats. Part of its grounds was taken for the building of Sallynoggin. It was demolished in 1978.

While most of the ROYAL MARINE HOTEL, Dun Laoghaire, may be said to have survived, its dramatic skyline with the high Victorian tower and French pavilions disappeared when the building was re-roofed about 1960. The original plan of 1863 called for a much larger building than that actually built. The architect, John McCurdy, scaled down the project, omitting a floor of bedrooms and substituting Italianate for gothic windows in an effort to cut the cost. In effect only the centrepiece and south wing of McCurdy's design were built, the old Hayes's Royal Hotel which stood to the north being remodelled rather than replaced.

While a contemporary report claimed that the scheme was truncated so as not to injure neighbouring Gresham Terrace, the collapse of the hotel company in 1867 suggests that the venture was never adequately financed. Its stylistic cousin, the Grand Hotel in Scarborough, failed two years earlier. In the 1970s the Royal Hotel section was re-

placed with a modern conference centre. Gresham Terrace, to the right in the photograph, which was built in the 1830s to the designs of Murray and Papworth, was demolished in 1974. The nine houses in the terrace had flat lead roofs, affording an excellent view of the harbour and bay.

THE PRIORY, RATHFARNHAM, a rather unassuming house, was the home of the celebrated lawyer and wit, John Philpot Curran. Formerly called Holly Park, it was purchased by him, with 35 acres, in 1790 when he moved from his native Newmarket, Co. Cork.

The original Priory was a cottage outside Newmarket built by Curran in 1786. Its name came from his position as Prior of the Order of St Patrick, or the Monks of the Screw founded by his friend Barry Yelverton (later Lord Avonmore), in 1779.

Two years after the move to Rathfarnham, Curran's daughter Gertrude, aged twelve, died following a fall from an upstairs window and was interred in the front lawn — in spite of Church opposition. Family life was difficult at the Priory, contributing to Curran's periodic bouts of melancholia. In 1793 Mrs Curran decamped with an impoverished clergyman. The house continued nevertheless as one of Dublin's most celebrated salons, with guests including such luminaries as Carleton, Scott, Yelverton, Wolfe and Toler (the hanging judge) commuting to the city by mule cart.

During 1798 troops were sent by Major Sirr to guard the Priory but were withdrawn by Wolfe, the Attorney General. Curran subsequently defended the United Irishmen. In 1803 Sirr was back again, this time with a search warrant. Young Sarah Curran was the betrothed of Robert Emmet, wanted on a charge of high treason. The father claimed to know of no such alliance. Emmet was subsequently arrested, not far away, at Harold's Cross. Although allegedly implicated by her correspondence with Emmet, Sarah escaped a sentence and was sent to friends in Cork where she married a Captain Sturgeon. She died in childbirth in 1808 in England.

John Philpot Curran was made Master of the Rolls, but was unsuited to the judiciary and resigned. He died at the Priory in 1817. The house survived into this century as a farm residence but was neglected for many years and was finally pulled down in the 1940s, the gravestone on the lawn having been destroyed in the early thirties.

OLD BAWN, Tallaght, was one of the earliest non-fortified houses built in the country. It was erected about 1635 in a 'wild and desolate spot' by William Bulkeley, Archdeacon of Dublin, who was granted the lands by Charles I in 1627. William's father, Launcelot, Archbishop of Dublin, was the younger son of Sir Richard Bulkeley of Beaumaris in Anglesey. Old Bawn was burnt in the insurrection of 1641. A claim was subsequently lodged for £3,000. It was rebuilt, and survived the Commonwealth. In the 1660s it was noted as having a household of thirty, and 'twelve hearths'. The late H. G. Leask has pointed out that there were in fact as many as fifteen — an early instance of tax evasion!

Archdeacon Bulkeley died in 1671 and was succeeded by his son Sir Richard, MP for Baltinglass. Old Bawn remained in the family (who later assumed the surname Tynte) until the late eighteenth century.

In Victorian times it was the residence of Joseph McDonnell, whose family operated the adjoining paper-mill. The house was joined to the mill and was partly mutilated in the process. The name Old Bawn is thought to relate to an earlier building on the site. The moat, some 20 feet wide, designed to keep out the marauding O'Byrnes and O'Tooles, was still discernible in outline when Leask surveyed the property in the early years of this century.

He speculated that the house, which had a typical late Tudor H-plan, was built by Welsh craftsmen imported by Bulkeley, and he noted that the splendid parlour mantelpiece dated 1635 had (like the staircase which it now accompanies in the National Museum) parallels at Plas Maur, Conway. Leask's contention (following Handcock) that the centrepiece of the elaborate plaster overmantel depicted the rebuilding of the walls of Jerusalem as described in Nehemiah, 'For the builders, every one had his sword girded by his side and with the other hand held a weapon, and so builded', while appropriate, was disputed by the late C. P. Curran on the grounds that only one of the many operatives is actually armed.

Old Bawn was apparently remodelled about 1700 when the staircase is thought to have been relocated and the pedimented entrance doorcase added. The outbuildings were also later, and were surmounted by a cupola and clock dated 1721. When Leask first visited Old Bawn in 1907, the fabric was relatively intact. When he returned six years later, demolition had already commenced. Today all that survives, outside the Museum, is the name — now a district in the Tallaght conurbation.

130

XI

NORTH EAST SUBURBS
AND COUNTY

In 1904 the ROYAL DUBLIN GOLF CLUB, then almost in its twentieth year, erected a new clubhouse: a two-storey timber frame building with brick chimney stacks and a tiled roof. The contractors were Messrs Boulton and Paul of Northampton who may have prefabricated the components. The new structure which replaced a small single-storey building was soon extended to cater for an increase in membership. The architect of the additions was Albert E. Murray, himself a keen golfer. On the night of 2 August 1943 the clubhouse was burnt to the ground, leaving nothing but the gaunt brick stacks standing. The difficulties of wartime necessitated the erection of a rather rudimentary replacement which served Royal Dublin for a number of years until their present clubhouse was completed.

Among Dublin's shortest lived churches was ST AIDAN'S on Drumcondra Road, built in an expanding suburb in the early years of this century and demolished in 1963. The perspective shows Richard Caulfeild Orpen's (1863–1938) 1901 design – that which was built. An alternative design incorporated a tower; the unfinished-looking stack and gables to the right of the nave were perhaps intended to form a base on which it might subsequently be raised. St Aidan's was part of St George's parish; a modern rectory now stands on its site.

Of the original eleven SWISS COTTAGES, mostly semi-detached, built by Lady Compton Domvile at Santry and completed in 1840, only two survive. The remainder have been destroyed piecemeal over the last thirty years. In 1878 Santry contained twenty-four houses described by Thom's as 'small but neatly built'. Seven of these cottages were in Schoolhouse Lane (the school dated from 1756).

Lady Domvile's model village also incorporated a post-office, a provision shop and a forge with a horseshoe door, all of which have disappeared. Picturesque model villages were much in vogue with early nineteenth-century landowners, Blaise Hamlet in Gloucestershire, designed by Nash in 1810–11, being perhaps the most celebrated.

Designs for Swiss cottages were to be found in all the pattern books of the day, notably those produced by P. F. Robinson and J. B. Papworth.

Some Irish proprietors commissioned Swiss cottages for their own use – i.e. Lisanoure, Co. Antrim (1829) by J. B. Keane, while the splendid Lough Bray, Co. Wicklow (1832) by William Vitruvius Morrison was erected for Surgeon-General Sir Philip Crampton, Bart. at the expense of the Lord Lieutenant, the Duke of Northumberland.

SANTRY COURT was erected in 1702 by the 3rd Lord Barry on or near the site of an earlier residence. It was substantially altered by Sir Charles Compton William Domvile in 1858. He had succeeded to the baronetcy in February 1857 on the death of his father. The alterations included moving the main entrance from one side of the house to the other — to what Domvile claimed was its original position. The new doorcase was copied from the original which he re-erected in the gardens. He appears to have employed Hugh Byrne as architect. Domvile also added a servants' wing, built an observation platform on the roof and converted an old stable to the south-west into an organ gallery, linked by a quadrant to the main house. The demesne covered 222 acres. Among the follies in his extensive gardens, landscaped by Ninian Niven (1799—1879), was an eighteenth-century hexagonal temple brought from his other seat at Templeogue, and an 'Eleanor cross' type pinnacle, erected in front of the entrance steps, commemorating an Arab stallion which Domvile, in a fit of rage, had had shot. Gas lamps lit the avenue and entrance court. The works at Santry and Templeogue, combined with land speculation in Killiney and Shankill, forced him into debt. He was declared bankrupt in 1875. The contents of Santry Court, valued at over £11,000 in 1872, were sold. The organ later went to a house in Mountjoy Square. The photographs of two of the drawing rooms, reproduced here, were taken by James Simonton some years earlier. The Domviles retained Santry Court until the late 1930s when it was acquired by Dublin Corporation who proposed to convert it into a mental home, attached to Grangegorman. It was burnt down while in use as a store during the war years and stood derelict until 1957 when it was demolished. The material was used as fill for the embankment around Santry Stadium. The entrance doorcase was salvaged and taken to the Royal Hospital. The main gates have been re-erected at Grangeforman, while the hexagonal garden temple is now at Luggala, Co. Wicklow. The remains of various monuments, gates and other fragments remain in the demesne.

Although the shell of TURVEY, close to Donabate, stands at the time of writing, the interiors have been so totally wrecked in the decade since this photograph was taken that this ancient seat of the Barnewall family must be regarded as lost.

The building history of Turvey is a complex one. It appears to have begun as a medieval tower house, only about 28 ft by 27 ft in the north-east corner, seen at the extreme right of the photograph. Turvey was granted to the Barnewalls by Thomas, Earl of Ormond, in 1560. A plaque which stood formerly over the garden gateway was inscribed 'The arms of Sir Christopher Barnewall and Dame Marian Sharle, alias Churley, who made this house in Anno Domini 1565'. The Elizabethan house appears to have been a southwards extension of the tower house and was allegedly constructed with stones from the nearby Grace Dieu nunnery, granted to the Barnewalls after the Dissolution.

The loss of eighteenth-century panelling on the first floor has revealed blocked-up windows, suggesting that the house was just one room wide. It was probably entered from the present basement level, and presented three gables to the east and one to the south — the three-window-wide section and lunette on the right in the photograph. The sections topped by the middle and left-hand lunette were in turn progressively added to the west to give an L-shaped house.

The Georgian doorway, with a richly carved tympanum topped by urns, is similar to that of Speaker Foster's house in Molesworth Street of the late 1720s (q.v.) and not unlike the back door of Shannongrove, Co. Limerick, dated 1723. It was added presumably by Henry Barnewall, 4th Viscount Kingsland, who succeeded in 1725. The major eighteenth-century alteration was the filling-in of the spaces between the gables to give a uniform flat parapet. A new roof with wide spans and flat apexes was then built above the level of the original. A staircase hall was added at the back, lit by a large Venetian window. One of the bricks in the elaborate quoins of this window was inscribed with the date 1773.

Henry died in the following year and was succeeded by his nephew George Barnewall, who conformed to the Established Church and took his seat in the House of Lords in 1787 as 5th Viscount Kingsland. He never lived at Turvey, which at the time of his succession had been rented to 'a sort of merchant banker' named Robert Birch, MP for Belturbet, who was declared bankrupt in 1785.

Some years later when it was rumoured that the 5th Viscount had died abroad, the house was claimed by Matthew Barnewall, a Dublin tavern waiter, who invited in friends and the local inhabitants in to celebrate his new-found fortune. He was evicted and imprisoned for contempt, but eventually, with a lawyer's help, was recognised as the 6th Viscount in 1814.

Turvey had in the intervening period passed to a cousin, Nicholas Barnewall, 14th Baron Trimblestown, who occupied the house until his death there in 1813. While it continued to devolve with the Trimblestown title, his successors preferred to rent it out rather than take up residence. Turvey was last occupied about 1970 when it was acquired by developers.

While KENURE PARK, Rush, owed its external appearance to George Papworth's refacing of 1842–56, behind his two ornate façades lay a large mid-eighteenth-century house which had retained its principal rooms. The best of these were the drawing-room which had a bow on the garden front and the room above it, in both of which was c.1750 plasterwork in the manner of Robert West. The staircase hall was largely Papworth's creation, with doric columns at ground level and ionic pilasters above, lit through painted glass panels beneath a central skylight.

The house was sold by Col. R. G. Fenwick-Palmer in 1964 and stood empty for some fourteen years, save for occasional occupation by film companies. Much deterioration occurred in the 1970s when it suffered from vandalism and neglect. In September 1978 it was town down in just two days. Following protests from local conservationists, Papworth's great corinthian portico was spared.

In 1835, the brothers Arthur and Benjamin Lee Guinness purchased 52 acres at Blackbush near Dollymount from John Venables Vernon of Clontarf Castle. The property included an eighteenth-century house known as Thornhill, previously occupied by Hugh O'Reilly. Two years later Benjamin married his cousin Elizabeth Guinness and acquired his brother's interest in the property, which he renamed ST ANNE'S, probably from an ancient holy well on the estate.

Benjamin is reputed to have demolished Thornhill and built anew. It seems more likely that he added to the old house. At some point, the stonework of the entrance door and fanlight were removed and re-erected in the garden.

The first documented improvement made by him was the erection of a sham ruin in the form of a bridge and tower over the entrance drive, to commemorate the birth of his first child Annie Lee in 1838. Other follies built in the pleasure grounds included a clock tower and a replica of a Herculanean house linked to a bridge over a stream known as the River Naniken. The stream was dammed just short of the foreshore to form a lake, the Crab Lake Water; at the edge of this he built a tea-house temple based on a Pompeian model. Closer to the mansion was a walled garden which incorporated a yew walk complete with statues brought back from Italy.

Benjamin was elected MP for Dublin in 1865, at which time he was engaged on the restoration of St Patrick's Cathedral; he was made a baronet two years

135

later. Sir Benjamin died in 1868 leaving an estate valued at over £1,100,000, the largest proved in Ireland to that date.

Further improvements had been made to the house proper, probably in the early 1860s, including the erection of a Richard Turner conservatory leading off the dining-room. The wing that splays to the left of the conservatory appears to have been part of the original house, albeit recased in Portland stone. The awkward angle, perhaps caused by a desire to give several rooms the best view of Dublin Bay, was even more apparent on the far (west) side of the house.

The plans which Sir Benjamin's successor, Sir Arthur Edward Guinness, embarked upon in 1873 set out to remedy this while effectively doubling the house in size. Money was no object. In 1876 he sold out his interest in the brewery to his younger brother Edward, later 1st Lord Iveagh, for £680,000, while in the eight years since his father's death he had received an income of £530,000. St Anne's was not to be the sole object of his attention. Improvements were made to his town house, 18 Leeson Street, while Ashford Castle, Cong, was greatly enlarged.

The work at St Anne's, which continued into the 1880s, included the creation of a new entrance wing parallel to the existing house and joined to the projecting section while masking the aforementioned angle. In the space between the new and old façades, Guinness's architect James Franklin Fuller placed a central hall and ballroom, double-storey height with a gallery supported on ionic columns, the shafts being of different kinds of Irish marble. To the left was a top-lit palm court rising to the full height of the building. A monumental staircase and a drawing-room complete with organ were built. Lady Guinness's boudoir received a ceiling based on an example at the Generaliffe, Granada taken from a plate in James Cavanah Murphy's *Arabian Antiquities of Spain*.

In 1880 Guinness was raised to the peerage as Baron Ardilaun. His arms, flanked by unicorns, were carved into the tympanum of the pediment over the new entrance. Much work was carried out on the demesne, with the creation of grand allées radiating from the house and flanked by oak and yew. On the axis of the new entrance he laid out a driveway, one and a half miles long. It would have been longer had he persuaded the owner of Furry Park to part with some of his land. Instead it had to kink to join the Howth Road. Another allée terminated with the spire of the new church, All Saints, Raheny, which Ardilaun commissioned from George Coppinger Ashlin who had replaced Fuller as estate architect. Lord Ardilaun died without issue in 1904.

The estate which had by this date grown to 460 acres passed to his widow and the baronetcy to a nephew. Lady Gregory wrote of Lady Ardilaun living in St Anne's in the 1920s, 'a lonely figure in her wealth, childless and feeling the old life shattered around her'. She died in 1925 leaving the bulk of her estate to her husband's nephew, the Right Reverend Benjamin John Plunket, Bishop of Meath. In her will she advised him to dismantle the house or reduce it to its pre-Ardilaun dimensions, stating, 'St Anne's is far too large and expensive for anyone to live in in the future. The enormous taxation and increase of wages and cost of everything will make it impossible.'

The Bishop moved in in 1926, erecting a plaque to his mother on the rustic arch put up by Sir Benjamin on her birth in 1838. In 1932 attempts were made to dispose of St Anne's and its 484 acres. Only two parties were interested, one of them Dublin Corporation who eventually in 1939 compulsorily acquired the house and estate for £55,000 of which all but £18,000 went to buy out the freehold and subsidiary interests.

A sale of contents, planned for October 1939, was advanced on the outbreak of war in September. Among the vast collection of art works and memorabilia sold was a reclining marble figure, 'The Shepherd Boy' by Hogan, acquired by a Dublin solicitor John Burke for £28 and presented to the nation. It is now in Iveagh House. St Anne's became a store for ARP equipment for the city. In December 1943 it was gutted by a fire which started in the east wing and quickly spread, destroying all but part of the entrance wing. The outer walls remained intact. However the ruins were vandalised and finally demolished in 1968. The park has been preserved as an amenity. The elaborate Tudor red-brick Ardilaun stables survive, as do most of the follies.

136

XII
UNBUILT DUBLIN

ST ANN'S CHURCH, DAWSON STREET. The parish of St Ann's was formed in 1707. Joshua Dawson gave a site (thought to be that of the present Royal Hibernian Hotel) which the parishioners found unsuitable and had exchanged for one on the east side of the street. The church was not begun until 1720 and it never received the ornate west end and steeple shown here in a plate from Brooking's Map (1728). There is a corresponding drawing in the Victoria and Albert Museum.

The architect was Isaac Wills, presumably the same man who acted as master-carpenter for Thomas Burgh at Steeven's Hospital. The design was, like St Werburgh's, based on Roman models. Maderno's Santa Susanna (1603) provided much of the inspiration for the façade, while the steeple draws on the flanking towers of Santa Agnese in the Piazza Navona by Borromini and others (1653 onwards).

A façade to a simplified design was begun but stopped a few feet short of the eaves of the church leaving an ugly buttressed gable to the nave behind. The curate's living quarters were on the upper level, over the porch.

In 1828, the architect William Murray (d.1849), Francis Johnston's cousin and successor, exhibited 'A Design for erecting a Tower and Spire on St Ann's Church, Dublin' at the Royal Hibernian Academy. Nothing happened until 1868, when the incomplete façade was taken down and replaced with a new front in the romanesque style designed by T. N. Deane. He also designed a spire which was never finished.

THE SOANE BANK: In 1799 the Governors of the Bank of Ireland asked the London architect (Sir) John Soane (1753–1837) to prepare designs for new premises on a triangular site bounded by College Street, D'Olier Street and Westmoreland Street. The Bank were dissatisfied with the unsuitable premises they had occupied in Mary's Abbey since their foundation sixteen years earlier, and, having failed to acquire the site of the old Custom House on Essex Quay, had taken an option on the College Street site from the Wide Street Commissioners.

Soane, who was architect to the Bank of England, a position obtained in 1788 through the influence of William Pitt, had had previous disappointments in Ireland. In 1780 he had travelled to Downhill in the mistaken belief that a vague offer from the Earl Bishop of Derry had constituted a commission. A house designed for Lady Granard was never built, while Baronscourt, which he extended in 1794, was burnt down two years later. The Wide Street Commissioners had been endeavouring to lay out Westmoreland and D'Olier Streets since before 1790, and following the Bank's decision they ordered new elevations to be prepared. Soane produced alternative schemes, which he appears to have worked on in London from October 1799. One was T-shaped, the other wedge-shaped to fit the site more practically. The latter, illustrated here, seems to have been the preferred solution. This perspective is dated 1 January 1800, while the other was done two months earlier. The buildings in the background are of course imaginary. Later in the year 1800 came the Act of Union.

Nothing further happened until 1802. On 17 August the secretary to the Bank wrote to Soane: 'I am ordered by the Governors and Directors . . . to express their obligation for your polite and disinterested conduct respecting the drawings for the Bank: which by the adoption of a Building already existing are rendered useless to them . . . they lament the intended exhibition . . . does not go forward, as those drawings must have done you much honour. . . . I am further directed . . . that in a few days the Bank purpose advertising for Plans for the alteration of the late Parliament House'. Once again Ireland had proved a disappointment. Soane had no further dealings with the Bank.

MUSEUM BUILDING, TRINITY COLLEGE: In 1833 a competition was held for a new building comprising hall, lecture rooms and museum in Front Square on the site of Richard Castle's campanile which had been taken down some forty years earlier. It was won by a Mr Payne, possibly George Richard Pain, of Cork. Second place went to William Deane Butler.

Yet it was Frederick Darley, appointed College architect about 1834, who received the commission. His designs were neither elaborate nor particularly inspired. However in 1836–7 he designed a further scheme, worked out in considerable detail and derived from Greek prototypes and the work of the German revivalists, in the manner of a secular temple with giant corinthian orders. There are close parallels with H. L. Elmes' slightly later designs for St George's Hall and Assize Courts in Liverpool. Had it been built it would have been Darley's masterpiece and perhaps the greatest Greek revival building in the country. As it turned out Trinity had to wait almost twenty years and hold another competition before it got its Museum.

138

On 20 June 1862 the foundation stone of the proposed CATHOLIC UNIVER-
SITY OF IRELAND was laid at Clonliffe with great ceremony. The plan was for
two quadrangles, one housing the university proper and the other being residen-
tial accommodation for three hundred students. The architect was J. J. McCarthy.
The design was Ruskinian and not unlike some of the entries for the Whitehall
Government Offices competition of 1857.

In 1864 a contractor was appointed and it seemed as if work was about to
commence. However, the project was abandoned and it was to be another
sixteen years before the second Dublin University opened—not at Clonliffe
but at Earlsfort Terrace. McCarthy designed the Church of the Holy Cross
College, Clonliffe, built by direct labour in 1873—5 and the subject of much
wrangling between him and his client Dr Verdon.

DUBLIN METROPOLITAN RAILWAY: In 1836, just two years after the opening of the country's first railway, the Dublin and Kingstown Company's engineer
Charles Blacker Vignoles (1793—1875) proposed a connecting railway running
between Westland Row and Watling Street to link with the projected line to the
south of Ireland. Vignoles' scheme called for bridges spanning D'Olier Street
and Westmoreland Street, going through a tunnel in the houses on each side.
The trains would be either towed by horse or by ropes connected to stationary
engines 'designed to consume their own smoke'. The section between Aston's
Quay and Watling Street was to be raised on an ionic colonnade above the quay
wall. Vignoles superimposed his proposal on a Petrie print. The scheme was put
to a parliamentary committee, but rejected.

In 1862 the idea of a bridge over the two streets was taken up anew by the
engineer Frederick Barry who also proposed building a Central Station and
monster hotel near Eustace Street. There was much opposition to the project.
The Corporation erected a dummy bridge across Westmoreland Street purport-
ing to show the effect of the railway. A piece of timber is said to have fallen
from the structure, killing a woman pedestrian. Barry's Bill passed the House of
Commons but was defeated in the Lords. At the next session he modified his
proposal to provide a tunnel under the two streets. Needless to say, neither this
nor any of the scores of connecting-railway projects concocted over the next
couple of decades ever got off the drawing-boards. It was not until 1891 that
the various termini were connected by the Loop Line.

139

GREEN STREET MARKET: In 1869, the *Irish Builder* published this view of a 'Proposed New Market on Green Street' designed by Edward Henry Carson (father of Lord Carson) for the site of the former Newgate Prison (q.v.).

The prison had closed about 1860 but was still standing disused six years later when the plan was shown on the Ordnance Survey map. Carson was probably employed by a private concern rather than by the municipal authorities. The nearby Anglesea Fruit Market, off Little Green Street, which the Corporation considered to be insanitary, was owned by a Dublin businesswoman.

The proposed new market was stillborn. In 1875 the Corporation finally succeeded in disposing of Newgate when they leased it to a consortium of fruit factors, Messrs Moran, Flanagan, O'Hanlon, Halpin and Byrne, for seventy-five years at £140 per annum. Twenty timber-framed stalls were erected within the walls of the gaol which had been reduced to single-storey height.

The venture does not appear to have been successful: by 1885 only William M. Byrne remained in occupation. By that date the Corporation were already planning their own markets for Mary's Abbey — designed by Spencer Harty and begun in 1888. A contemporary photograph shows a James North 'To Be Let' notice fixed to the gates of the Newgate market. The site was cleared by the Corporation in 1899 to create St Michan's Park.

McCurdy and Mitchell were among the ten firms invited to submit entries in the SOUTH CITY MARKETS competition of 1878. Their design 'Pro Bono Publico' was unplaced. Apart from the winners (q.v.) only two other designs are known — Messrs O'Neill and Byrne's 'Con Amore' which was runner-up, and Sir Thomas Drew's 'Simplex', both of which were published in the architectural press.

The *Freeman's Journal* described 'Pro Bono Publico' as being 'in the Queen Anne style with central pavilions in the principal fronts and lofty dormers'. The *Building News* praised the plan and noted that 'the exterior, as shown by a cleverly-handled perspective drawing, tinted in sepia and indigo, presents a very picturesque effect. It is a little flat in treatment but no doubt with the effect of coloured materials much of the flatness would disappear.'

In the late nineteenth century a number of projects were designed for TRINITY COLLEGE which stylistically rejected the established classicism on the campus, harkening back to its Elizabethan foundations. Among these were William Mansfield Mitchell's 'Proposed New Chambers' for the site of the Rubrics, which owed something to the competition design that he had entered, with his later partner John McCurdy, for the South City Markets in 1879.

The design predates the filling in of the Library colonnade by Sir Thomas Drew in 1889. There is an interesting Bridge of Sighs link to the first floor of the Library. T. N. Deane had designed a bridge linking the Library to the Museum in 1878, in the Italian Renaissance style: the project was fortunately stillborn. In the event the Rubrics were remodelled rather than replaced in 1894. The commission, however, did not go to Mitchell but to R. J. Stirling. The College finally got a neo-Elizabethan block with Drew's Graduates Memorial Building, 1901—3, which was selected in preference to designs by both Deane and Stirling.

THE LYCEUM THEATRE: In 1884, one James Dillon, acting for London interests, was granted a patent of limited duration for the erection of a 2,500-seat theatre to be sited at the junction of the newly made Tara Street and Brunswick Street, the site of the present fire station. Elaborate plans were prepared by a Dublin architect, Arthur Dudgeon, about whom little is known.

While the Theatre Royal had been destroyed by fire four years earlier, the proprietor Michael Gunn had replaced it with a music hall, the Leinster Hall, rather than a legitimate theatre. However, in 1887 Gunn decided to apply for a patent. Three years later both proposals came up before the Solicitor General at Dublin Castle. Doubts were expressed about the financial resources of the Lyceum, whose promoter was a Mr Paetow of London. He pleaded that the theatre could be commenced within six months and built within two years. One month's extension only was granted and the project collapsed. Dudgeon's beautifully detailed drawings survive as testimony to Dublin's loss. The revamped Leinster Hall reopened in 1897 as the Theatre Royal (q.v.).

THE LANE GALLERY: The site chosen by Hugh Lane for his Municipal Gallery of Modern Art must rank among the most unusual ever considered for a Dublin public building. In 1912 he had his architects Sir Edwin Lutyens (1869–1944) prepare designs for a gallery spanning the Liffey on the site of the Metal Bridge (erected 1816). While no one objected to the removal of the then little regarded bridge now known to have been designed by John Windsor of the Coalbrookedale Iron Works) many opposed the location, and their objections lost Dublin Lane's picture collection also.

The idea of a gallery originated in 1902 when Lane, a successful London art dealer and the son of a Cork clergyman, organised an exhibition of old masters at the Royal Hibernian Academy. Two years later he was asked to assemble works by contemporary Irish artists for the Louisiana Purchase Exhibition at St Louis (see Jeanne Sheehy's *The Rediscovery of Ireland's Past*, London 1980). This proved abortive, but he succeeded in bringing the paintings to London where they were exhibited at the Guildhall. Lane broached the idea of a modern art gallery for Dublin, and obtained on approval a number of nineteenth-century French paintings from two important private collections; he also donated several from his own collection, and he exhibited all of these at the RHA and later at the National Museum.

While he succeeded in his plan of getting patrons (among them the Prince and Princess of Wales and President Theodore Roosevelt) to purchase paintings for the Gallery, his enthusiasm was resented in some circles. The Gallery opened in Clonmell House, Harcourt Street in 1908 and was supported by the Gaelic League amongst others. However, Lane had made it a condition of the loan that the Corporation build a permanent home for the collection. In January 1913 they voted £22,000.

Lane had to find a site and raise the balance of £43,000. Among the sites considered were that of the former skating rink on Earlsfort Terrace (q.v.), rejected when he saw what the University proposed to erect beside him – the old Turkish Baths from Lincoln Place (q.v.) – Lord Edward Street, Merrion Square and St Stephen's Green. Lutyens designed alternative schemes for the latter; the Gallery was to face the College of Surgeons. However this was rejected by Lord Ardilaun who had given the Green to the city, and was attacked by William Martin Murphy, proprietor of the *Irish Independent*, who had previously praised Lane's efforts, on the grounds that 'fresh air was a more desirable asset for the people than French art'.

An architect named Frank Craig suggested the Liffey site, for which no land was needed, and Lane was delighted with it. Although R. C. Orpen, who had been advising him on locations, was less enthusiastic, Lane proceeded to have Lutyens prepare drawings. The Corporation accepted the proposal initially, then rejected it and its English architect. Lane refused to revise his plans and promptly withdrew his paintings from Clonmell House, changing his will to bequeath the collection to the London National Gallery. He later recanted, and added the famous codicil leaving the pictures to Dublin but failed to have it witnessed. He died several months after in the *Lusitania* sinking. Dublin failed to get the paintings during the legal wrangles which followed, and even today has to share them with London.

142

In 1912 a competition, limited to ten invited architects, was held for new CIVIC OFFICES for Dublin Corporation. The site was on Lord Edward Street next to Newcomen's Bank. Several competition entries survive. The winning design by L. A. McDonnell (d. 1925) of McDonnell and Reid, which had a tower based on San Carlo alla Quattro Fontane in Rome, is reproduced here. In 1917, McDonnell again employed this motif for his Bank of Ireland in Lower O'Connell Street.

In 1939 Abercrombie and Kelly produced their second city plan for the Corporation's town planning committee, published two years later. This included a proposed city and county administration building on a site to the west side of a widened Parliament Street, with an L-shaped wing running along Essex Quay.

In 1955 Messrs Jones and Kelly prepared a design for a site located further west, on Wood Quay. A photograph of their model is illustrated here. Nothing further happened until 1969 when another competition was held, again for the Wood Quay site. The winning entry of Stephenson Gibney Associates is currently under construction to a modified design.

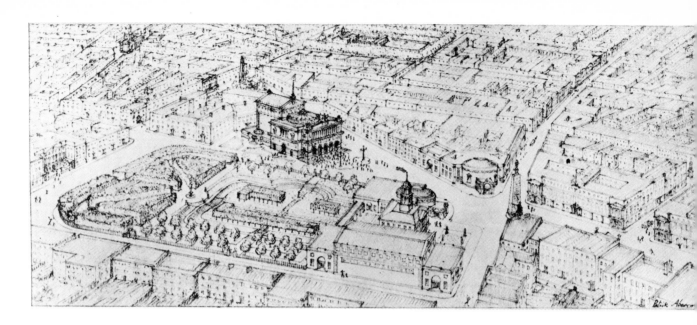

Among Patrick Abercrombie and Sydney and Arthur Kelly's prize-winning proposals (submitted in 1914) for *Dublin of the Future* were the erection of two important public buildings: a ROMAN CATHOLIC CATHEDRAL and a NATIONAL THEATRE. The site of the former was to be opposite the Technical College in Bolton Street, with a Florentine façade facing down Capel Street. Behind the cathedral was to have been a piazza which would have necessitated the demolition of Henrietta Street.

The King's Inns was to have been incorporated in the composition while a stylised Irish round tower campanile would stand on the axis of the cathedral. The Broadstone received happier treatment as the set piece at the edge of a new circus on the Phibsborough Road.

The theatre, combining features culled from such diverse sources as Schinkel and Garnier, was earmarked for a site in Cavendish Row and would have dominated the vista down O'Connell Street. The outbreak of war delayed the adjudication until October 1916 when Abercrombie and Kelly received first prize. Their plan was not published until 1922. In their report the adjudicators wrote, 'It is, of course, clearly to be understood that although as adjudicators we are unanimous as to the above award and honourable mentions, we are not thereby endorsing, as Town Planners, all or any of the particular proposals of this series of plans or solving the problems of Greater Dublin; nor are we recommending their being put into execution to the exclusion of all other alternatives.'

THE IRISH HOSPITALS TRUST began in June 1930 in two houses in Earlsfort Terrace. Rapid expansion in the following years saw prize distributions rise from an initial £400,000 to several million pounds over the three annual draws. In December 1937 work commenced on a 96,000 sq. ft single storey building to house a projected 4,000 clerks.

The main structure, designed by J. J. Robinson, was completed by March 1939. Lit only by northlights, it was air-conditioned and had among other innovations a compressed air system for vacuum cleaning. Plans were made for a further addition to house the sweeps draw which had hitherto been held in the Plaza, Middle Abbey Street (q.v.), and at the Mansion House, in a vast art deco hall surmounted by a tower that would have looked more at home on Sunset Boulevard than the Merrion Road. A huge model was made and transported across Dublin on a trailer to the 1938 Silver Jubilee Draw at the Mansion House.

The outbreak of war and ensuing decline in receipts prevented the project from reaching fruition.

The proposals made in 1945 for a THOMAS DAVIS MEMORIAL in St Stephen's Green designed by Raymond McGrath (1903—77) featured a central fountain on the spot formerly occupied by the statue of George II (q.v.). The carved pavilions which flanked it and were each intended to house a pair of statues in the colonnade were in some respects reminiscent of neoclassical monuments of the 1930s. Their sombre aspect was in contrast to the light-hearted scene in the picture. An alternative memorial site was selected in College Green, previously the home of William III (q.v.) and a foundation stone was laid on 12 September 1945 by President Sean T. O'Kelly. It was to be another twenty years, however, before the Davis statue and ensemble by Edward Delaney would be erected.

In April 1964 an all-party committee met to discuss the JOHN F. KENNEDY
MEMORIAL HALL, a project initiated by the government to commemorate the
late President. The idea of a concert hall had been suggested by the Arts Council.
A proposal to erect such a building as early as 1946 on the site of the Rotunda
gardens was abandoned following a change of government. In 1952 a private
company had been formed by music enthusiasts to promote a concert and
assembly hall.

Raymond McGrath, who was then principal architect of the Office of Public
Works, was entrusted with the Kennedy Hall. The consultants included Professor
Lothar Cremer, an acoustics expert, who had worked on the Philharmonie and
Deutsche Oper in Berlin, and organ builder Ralph Downes.

The committee considered six sites, among them St Anne's Park in Raheny
(q.v.), and finally settled on a 14½ acre site at Beggar's Bush Barracks in Haddington Road, already in state hands and close to the city centre. It would run
from Shelbourne Road to Northumberland Road where some houses were to
be demolished. A new National Library and a tower block to house the Depart-
ments of Social Welfare and Health were, for a time, also proposed for the site.

The Kennedy Hall was to comprise a large hall capable of seating two thousand,
and a smaller auditorium seating five hundred. A Kennedy Memorial Room to
exhibit memorabilia was to be accommodated in the foyer. In March 1965
Raymond McGrath's plans were published. They were revised by February 1966.
The final scheme (illustrated here) had crisp classical lines in place of the more
faddish battered walls of the original. Tender drawing stage was reached by
January 1970. In May of the following year there were suggestions that the
concert hall be sited in the Phoenix Park, to the west of the Wellington Testi-
monial. In April 1974 the government decided not to proceed with the erection
of a new building but instead to convert the Great Hall of University College,
Dublin, at Earlsfort Terrace, built originally as part of Alfred Gresham Jones's
Exhibition Building of 1865. At the time of writing this project is nearing
completion.

Glossary

ANTHEMION: Classical ornament based on honeysuckle flower and leaves.

ARCHITRAVE: The lowest member of the classical entablature — that is, the horizontal members above a column. Also used to describe the ornamental moulding running around the curve of an arch: and the mouldings around door and window openings.

ASHLAR: Hewn stone used for the facings of walls, laid in horizontal courses with vertical joints.

BATTER: Term applied to walls built out of the upright, or gently sloping inwards.

BAY: Vertical division of a wall between windows, buttresses or other features in the same plane. Quadrangular space between beams in a timber roof or principal divisions in a vaulted roof and consequently compartment of the room below.

BAWN: Enclosure surrounding or adjoining a castle or plantation house.

BREAKFRONT: Centrepiece of façade projecting slightly forward of the main wall plane and rising through its full height.

CARYATIDS: Name given to statues of women, employed as columns, in Grecian architecture as in the Erechtheum at Athens.

COMPO: Abbreviation of 'composition' — i.e. cement render applied to external walls particularly used in the nineteenth century to describe various patented compositions.

CORBEL: Short piece of timber or stone projecting from a wall to carry a weight above it — i.e. balcony, roof eaves etc.

CORNICE: Strictly speaking the upper part of the classical entablature, but more commonly used to describe the highest course or suit of moulding projecting from a wall. Internally, the highest moulding in the angle between walls and ceiling.

COURSE: A single range or horizontal row of stones or bricks in the wall of a building.

COVE: Arched or sloped moulding in the angle between walls and ceiling.

CROCKETS: Flower or foliage decoration projecting at regular intervals from the angles of spires, canopies, pinnacles and gables.

ENGAGED COLUMNS: Columns attached to or partly sunk into a wall.

ENTABLATURE: The superstructure which lies horizontally upon the columns in classical architecture — divided into three parts — architrave, frieze and cornice.

FINIAL: An ornament which crowns a pinnacle, canopy, pediment or gable.

GLOSSARY *Continued*

FLÈCHE:	A spire, usually a wooden metal-sheathed spire fixed to the roof ridge.
FOOTINGS:	Projecting course or courses of wall foundations.
GIANT ORDER:	Order whose columns or pilasters rise from the ground through two or more storeys.
HEXASTYLE:	Six-columned portico.
LUNETTE:	Semicircular window, opening or tympanum.
MODILLION:	Ornament resembling a bracket, employed in series to support the upper member of a corinthian or composite cornice.
ORIEL:	A window projecting from the face of the wall, frequently resting on brackets or corbel heads.
PERISTYLE:	A range of columns surrounding a building or part of a building, i.e. the drum beneath a dome or a colonnade around a courtyard or square.
PILASTER:	A flat pillar or pier placed against a wall.
PUTTO (PUTTI):	Representation of a usually naked small child in plasterwork etc.
QUADRANT WALLS:	Curving walls joining projecting wings of a building to the central block.
QUOINS:	Stones put in the angles of buildings to strengthen them or plaster decoration simulating same.
ROCOCO STYLE:	Light and elegant decorative style regarded by some as the last phase of the baroque rather than an independent style. Seen in Dublin in the plasterwork of Robert West and his school.
RUBBLE MASONRY:	Rough unhewn stones, usually laid uncoursed, traditionally as a backing behind ashlar or as a facing with cut stone dressings.
RUSTICATION:	Masonry worked with grooves between the courses to give the appearance of open joints, often reserved as a facing for the lower floors of a building.
TETRASTYLE:	Four-columned portico.
TRUSS:	In carpentry, a frame of timber constructed so as to combine lightness with strength and used to support loads or span openings as in a roof.
TYMPANUM:	Flat surface or space within a pediment and also the surface between the top of a door and the arch over it.

Indexes
INDEX OF PLACES

INDEX OF ARCHITECTS, ARTISTS AND CRAFTSMEN

NOTES ON SOME ARCHITECTS

1.   Richard Castle: Some accounts give his name as Cassel or Cassels. German born, it would appear that his surname was originally Castles (or Cassels) de Richardi which he shortened to Castle.

2.   The Deane family: There were three Thomas Deanes — father, son and grandson, all of whom were knighted. Sir Thomas Deane (1792-1870) practised in Cork and only moved to Dublin while in semi-retirement some nine years before his death. He was knighted in 1830 during his second term of office as High Sheriff of Cork. His son and partner, Sir Thomas Newenham Deane, usually known as T. N. Deane (1828-99) moved to Dublin in 1854 with the third partner. Tullamore-born Benjamin Woodward (1816-61). T. N. was knighted in 1890 on the completion of the National Museum and National Library. His son Sir Thomas Manly Deane (1851-1933) joined the practice in 1878 and was knighted in 1911 for his role as superintending architect of the College of Science complex.

3.   The Murray family: William Murray (d.1849) took over the practice of his cousin Francis Johnston on the latter's death in 1829. He was in turn succeeded by his son William George Murray (1822/3-1871) who was followed by his son Albert Edward Murray (1849-1924).